Contemporary
Federal Policy
Toward
American Indians

**Recent Titles in
Contributions in Ethnic Studies**

From Paddy to Studs: Irish-American Communities in the Turn of the
Century Era, 1880 to 1920
Timothy J. Meagher, editor

Hibernia America: The Irish and Regional Cultures
Dennis Clark

Strategies for Survival: American Indians in the Eastern United States
Frank W. Porter III, editor

Race, Ethnicity, and Minority Housing in the United States
Jamshid A. Momeni, editor

Creative Awakening: The Jewish Presence in Twentieth-Century American
Literature, 1900–1940s
Louis Harap

The South African Society: Realities and Future Prospects
Human Sciences Research Council

In the Mainstream: The Jewish Presence in Twentieth-Century American
Literature, 1950s–1080s
Louis Harap

Dramatic Encounters: The Jewish Presence in Twentieth-Century American
Drama, Poetry, and Humor and the Black-Jewish Relationship
Louis Harap

The Politics of Racial Inequality: A Systematic Comparative Macro-Analysis
from the Colonial Period to 1970
J. Owens Smith

How Minority Status Affects Fertility: Asian Groups in Canada
Shivalingappa S. Halli

Religion, Intergroup Relations, and Social Change in South Africa
Human Sciences Research Council

Latino Empowerment: Progress, Problems, and Prospects
*Roberto E. Villareal, Norma G. Hernandez, and Howard D. Neighbor,
editors*

Contemporary Federal Policy Toward American Indians

EMMA R. GROSS

Contributions in Ethnic Studies, Number 25
LEONARD W. DOOB, SERIES EDITOR

GREENWOOD PRESS
New York • Westport, Connecticut • London

Library of Congress Cataloging-in-Publication Data

Gross, Emma R.
   Contemporary federal policy toward American Indians / Emma R.
Gross.
      p. cm.—(Contributions in ethnic studies, ISSN 0196–7088 ;
no. 25)
   Bibliography: p.
   Includes index.
   ISBN 0–313–26505–4 (lib. bdg. : alk. paper)
   1. Indians of North America—Government relations.   I. Title.
II. Series.
E93.G87   1989
323.1'197'073—dc19   88–38188

British Library Cataloguing in Publication Data is available.

Library of Congress Catalog Card Number: 88–38188
ISBN: 0–313–26505–4
ISSN: 0196–7088

First Published in 1989

Greenwood Press, Inc.
88 Post Road West, Westport, Connecticut 06881

Printed in the United States of America

The paper used in this book complies with the
Permanent Paper Standard issued by the National
Information Standards Organization (Z39.48–1984).

10 9 8 7 6 5 4 3 2 1

Copyright Acknowledgment

Excerpt taken from the *Washington Representatives* (1979), published by Columbia
Books, Inc. of Washington, D.C., appears by permission of Columbia Books.

This book is dedicated to those policy specialists who gave so unstintingly of their time and opinions.

Contents

Tables and Figure   ix

Series Foreword   xi

Preface   xiii

Introduction   xv

1.   The Failure of American Indian Policy: History's Verdict   1

2.   The Constitutional Mandate on Indian Affairs and the Role of Law   15

3.   The Origins of Self-Determination Ideology and Constitutional Sovereignty   31

4.   Federal Spending and Indian Self-Determination   49

5.   Presidential Initiative and Indian Policy Development   61

6.   Congressional Advocacy in Indian Affairs   75

7.   The Indian Influence on Policy Development in the 1970s   93

8.   The Future of American Indian Politics   107

Appendix A.   Note on Method   117

Appendix B.   Landmark Indian Legislation, 1970 to 1980   121

Appendix C.   Washington Representatives: Firms Listing
     Two or More American Indian Clients, Tribes, and/or
     Organizations in 1983   123

Selected Bibliography   127

Index   141

Tables and Figure

TABLES

2.1	Sources of Legal and Statutory Influence on Indian Policy Development	16
3.1	Policy Specialists' Definitions of Self-Determination Ideology	33
4.1	The Influence of Federal Spending on Indian Policy Development	50
5.1	Sources of Presidential Influence	62
6.1	Sources of Congressional Influence on Indian Policy Development	76
7.1	Sources of Indian and Friend of Indian Influence on Indian Policy Development	94
A.1	Number of Respondents by Race and Type of Interview	118

A.2   Respondent Profiles: Experience, Education,
       Occupation   119

FIGURE

3.1   Perspectives on Self-Determination   32

Series Foreword

Contributions in Ethnic Studies focuses on the problems that arise when people from different cultures and with different goals come together and interact, either productively or tragically. The modes of adjustment or conflict are various, but usually one group dominates or attempts to dominate the other. Eventually, some accommodation is reached, but the process is likely to be long and, for the weaker group, painful. No one scholarly discipline monopolizes the research necessary to comprehend these intergroup relations. The emerging analysis, therefore, is of interest to historians, social scientists, social workers, and psychiatrists.

Most of us are acquainted with the one-sided accommodations originally sought and achieved by European settlers throughout the continental United States with reference to native Indians. First, the aim was to exterminate them in battles and then eventually to quarter the survivors in reservations. Whether from anthropological studies, travellers, fictional or semifictional accounts offered in books and motion pictures, we have also obtained insight into the enduring customs and values of these somewhat heterogeneous Indian tribes—or societies as we now properly and more accurately call them. During the recent period vividly and meticulously reported in this book, we can learn how and why there has been "a genuine turning point in the political future of the American Indian." Instead of being exploited or ignored and in spite of backlashes by the privileged whites and other setbacks, Indians and their ways of life have come to be respected. And the Indians themselves must now decide the extent to which they would retain some of their ancient ways or become more or less like the rest of Americans in this multiethnic country.

On the basis of a meticulous examination of public documents and after interviewing 66 Indian and non-Indian persons—"policy specialists" who are "knowledgeable about Indian policy" and most of whom have legal degrees—the author provides a detailed history of the changes in American policy during the last two decades. She isolates and analyzes the numerous legal points that have been invoked and that have been the guides: the American Constitution, federal and state laws, local ordinances, the 650 treaties with American Indians, court decisions, and suits initiated by Indians and their opponents. Lobbyists on behalf of change and no change have bombarded Washington. The role of American presidents has often been critically important. Indian organizations have been active with occasional demonstrations and successes on behalf of Red Power. The "devastating impact of federal policy" and present improvements are recounted. The conscience, ruthlessness, and ethnocentrism of Americans at large, fluctuating among the varying values of exploiting them, protecting them, cutting them adrift, trusting them as sovereign entities, assimilating them, and demanding their lands, have affected governmental policies. The views of scholars are likewise cited because they have had access to power.

The author's analysis is of interest on several compelling scores. She offers a history of Indian policies within recent years. She isolates many of the forces and ideologies that have determined those policies. She makes one think not only about American Indians but also about other minorities (and for that matter about the majorities in South Africa and Burundi) who have been or are being mistreated by those in power. Our existence as individual persons or as members of a group is thus both recalled and challenged over and beyond our native Indians.

Leonard W. Doob
Series editor

Preface

Many of the ideas presented in this study have benefited from the helpful comments of friends, colleagues, students, and especially, anonymous reviewers. Papers based on some of the findings discussed in this book were presented to audiences at the American Indian Policy Conference, the American Indian Studies Center, at the University of California at Los Angeles (February 1985), and at the Annual Program Meeting of the Council on Social Work Education, Atlanta, Georgia (March 1988). I am grateful for these opportunities and for the friendly advice and warm support I've received from these sources.

I would especially like to thank Eunice Shatz, former dean of the Graduate School of Social Work at the University of Utah. Her willingness to make additional resources available to me made collecting the interview data possible. I am also indebted to John Kingdon, Rosemary Sarri, Zeke Hasenfeld, and Jack Walker of the University of Michigan, who provided wise counsel and set high standards for me to follow.

Finally, I am very appreciative for the wizardry of my typists, Kay Durrant and Carolyn Bennion.

Introduction

Scholars have long been of the opinion that American Indian-federal relations are a study in the failure of democratic processes to protect and enhance the interests and well-being of American Indian tribes and communities. This conclusion has been based on the observation that minority populations are generally viewed as not well-represented by American governmental institutions, especially when their interests come into conflict with those of the majority. In fact, fairly soon after contact with the white Europeans who settled the North American continent, American Indian populations—by virtue of war, disease, and disenfranchisement—did become a minority in the sense that their populations were decimated. Even by the most generous estimates, today Indian people number fewer than two million and they continue to suffer from extreme poverty.[1]

In the second place, Indian constituencies clearly do not influence electoral outcomes at either local or national levels and are thus also a minority in this respect. It would seem, therefore, that James Madison was right to worry about the ability of a democracy based on the rule of the majority to fairly represent political minorities. Most students of American Indian history would agree that this has been the case.

Chapter 1 examines the conclusion that American Indian policy has been a failure. Among other things, this argument points out that the trust relationship—America's historical obligation to honor the treaties and protect Indian interests—has been frequently set aside by the federal government in its pursuit of manifest destiny and the public interest. From this vantage point, the federal government's desire to acquire American Indian lands and natural resources is thus said to lead to policy decisions that are predictably exploitive, and harmful, to the interests of Indian populations. Accordingly, manifest destiny, public interest, and even racist ideologies have been used to justify governmental actions that would otherwise be viewed as unconscionable (Horsman, 1981). Criticism of American Indian policy has thus emphasized its ethnocentric, paternalistic, and acquisitive nature. In adopting a "we know what is best for you" attitude in behalf of an ill-defined public interest, American society, through the federal government, has succeeded in divesting Indian populations of most of their property and in stunting their social, economic, and political growth. These are powerful and convincing arguments. Together, they appear to explain American Indian-federal relations until well into the twentieth century.

This book, however, presents an alternative thesis. Sometime during the 1970s, a liberal shift occurred in Indian policy-making so that Indian constituency interests came to be surprisingly well-represented in major legislation enacted at the time. This study attempts to explain how and why this fundamental shift in Indian policy took place at that time. The assertion, however, that American Indians have ever succeeded in having their policy preferences translated into law is understandably greeted with disbelief. At best, it is paradoxical that a population rightly viewed as oppressed historically, and in the present, might in any sense have transcended the limits of its oppression. If it is possible to become less oppressed by becoming politically enfranchised, however, then it is in this sense that Indian tribes and organizations came to be represented in the policy arena of the 1970s. Several other observations about the theoretical framework adopted in this study will also help put this thesis into perspective.

This study is emphatically not a history of Indian-white policy relations. No attempt is made, as the historian might, to argue that the patterns and continuities of past times significantly alter or explain events in the present. Neither is the theoretical perspective employed in this study ahistorical, however. Thus, the problematic history of Indian-federal relations constitutes the backdrop against which many of the policy issues of the 1970s were defined. Indeed, the enactment of most of the policies examined in this study—whether land and natural resources or social welfare related—was importantly influenced by a desire to make right the wrongs of past policies, which admittedly violated treaties and the trust relationship.

Rather, this is a public policy study. As such, it tries to answer the questions originally posed by Harold Laswell: Who gets what, when, and how? The "who" of this approach are American Indians. The "what" is a question about the distribution and redistribution of national resources and what was allocated to Indian populations. The "when" seeks to establish why resources were distributed as they were during the 1970s, and the "how" examines the legislative and executive institutional decision-making processes that resulted in the enactment of federal policies favorable to Indian interests. Thus, the framework for public policy analysis adopted is cross-sectional rather than longitudinal. It examines a slice—the decade of the seventies—of American Indian policy history and focuses exclusively on the dynamics of policy-making. My interest, in other words, is to show why policy-makers chose to consider and enact the policies they did and why they did not ignore Indian interests, as they otherwise might have.

The literature of political science is replete with examples of similar attempts to explain why and how policymakers vote as they do, when they do. Many of these studies concentrate on identifying the principles that underlie decision-making processes. Others focus on revealing the factors that influence choices. Yet others attempt to explain what characteristics of specific policies indicate the likelihood that legislators will respond in one way and not another. Some even seek to explain why certain problems do not reach the public agenda in the first place.

Whatever their special angle or approach to the problem, however, most students of public policy share the belief that policy may be differentiated into separate phases or stages for the purposes of facilitating scholarly analysis and explaining how policies are made and carried out. Accordingly, I have adopted a theoretical perspective defining the public policy process as composed of four stages: agenda-setting, or the process by which public concerns reach policy-making arenas; policy development, or formulation—by which issues are turned into legislation and enacted; policy implementation, or those processes by which legislative statutes are carried out; and, policy evaluation, or the means employed to judge how well the law has been carried out in terms of its original intents and purposes. For this study, I have chosen to investigate the processes associated with the development or formulation of Indian policy. Therefore, this is not a study that primarily seeks to determine how questions of importance to Indian populations reach the public agenda, nor about how or how well policies are carried out once they are enacted.

It is important to point out that the choice I have made to examine policy development, rather than implementation or evaluation, both qualifies my thesis and defines its signal limitation. In other words, I talk about how Indian policy is formulated and enacted, and not about whether these policies are effective, useful, or desirable, either in terms of their impact on Indian populations or with respect to competing ideologies. Thus, the dependent variable in this study is policy development. I am interested in explaining how Indian policy is made, not how it is carried out.

The debate about whether Indian policy is good or bad continues unresolved and the findings presented here will not decide the question. Probably nothing will. Students of Indian affairs will disagree about what is in the best interests of either the U.S. or Indian populations, as long as limited resources are at stake and ideological differences remain as central to the debate as they are at present. What this study does accomplish is to shed some light on how Indian policy is made and, by extension, to suggest how policy entrepreneurs can act in order to see to it that their own interests are enhanced. Thus, the study is limited because it does not pronounce upon the effectiveness or value of the policies examined. These, in their turn, are questions about which there is much debate and disagreement. Implementation and evaluation analyses remain to be done.

Given the framework of analysis from which the questions addressed in this study are approached, and the caveat that this investigation does not try to determine the effectiveness of Indian policy, a word about the propositions to be examined completes this introduction to the study. I have already referred to one of these propositions: that federal policy-making processes are not democratic and representative with respect to minority interests. Alternatively, I have asked: (a) whether Indian constituencies have special access and input into federal policy-making processes, and if so, what difference such access makes, and (b) whether the dynamics of Indian policy-making resemble or are different from those that describe policy-making processes in other issue areas.

In order to examine these questions, two theories common to public policy analysis can be applied to the study of Indian affairs; first, the constitutional or "classical" model and second, the interest group model.[2,3] Briefly, they serve the present analysis for several reasons. The classical model is useful because there is a constitutional mandate—Article I, Section 8, Clause 3, and Article II, Section 2, Clause 2, and the treaties—which provides legal and political justification for the federal government's authority over Indian tribes and populations. At the same time, however, it can be argued that the constitutional model has failed to protect and promote the well-being of Indian populations, thus calling into question its ability to extend democratic principles to the Indian. The constitutional mandate on Indian affairs is examined in Chapter 2.

Alternatively, the interest group model offers a different explanation for understanding Indian politics. Recent interest group theory indicates that allocative decisions about public resources—distributive, redistributive, and regulatory, for example—tend to favor those special interests who are best able to represent themselves (Hayes, 1978; Lowi, 1964, 1966; Price, 1978).[4] Intuitively, one would immediately suppose that Indian constituencies have not been able to successfully represent themselves in this sense. There is no evidence, for example, that formal Indian organizations have ever effectively mobilized in behalf of Indian policy goals and preferences. On the other hand, there is reason to believe that Indians, like other minorities, may have benefited from the political strategies and social movements of the civil rights era of the 1960s and, thus, that their activism might have had an impact on policy development (Morris, 1984; Peroff, 1982; Taylor, 1983).[5] Thus, interest group theory complements constitutional theory when explaining Indian policy development during the 1970s.

The idea that Indians might have benefited from civil rights ideologies and strategies was tested through related propositions: (a) that, during the 1970s, self-determination ideology was operationally defined in such a way that, for the most part, both Indian and non-Indian interests could support the policy-making strategies implied by it, and (b) that Indian and Indian advocacy organizations were sufficiently well-organized during the seventies to have a decisive impact on Indian policy.

With respect to the idea that self-determination ideology makes a difference in policy-making, I postulate that self-determination was defined along a continuum. At one end were those definitions emphasizing granting Indian populations greater legal and political sovereignty, such as those defining political jurisdiction or expanding the land base of Indian tribes. At the other end of the continuum were those definitions centered around obtaining greater participation for Indians in policy-making processes or more freedom in deciding the internal affairs of Indian tribes (self-government). Chapter 3 presents the findings on this question.

The second proposition, that Indian interests will influence policy-making when they are well-organized, is discussed throughout and examined in Chapter 7. Thus, resource rich organizations—those that possessed effective leadership, membership incentives, and the physical and financial resources to carry out their objectives—were most likely to see their policy preferences enacted into law. In fact, it may be argued that government funding of Indian organizations in the late sixties and early seventies, as well as the political actions taken by wealthier Indian nations and "friend of the Indian" organizations, contributed to the establishment of effective Indian interest groups (Hertzberg, 1971; Josephy, 1984; Prucha, 1973; Walker, 1983).

Finally, there were several other, unexpected, findings that affirmed the significance of additional factors influencing Indian policy development. Chapter 4 looks at how federal spending and the war on poverty favored Indian interests. Chapter 5 discusses the crucial role played by presidential initiative and support on Indian policy development, in particular that of the Nixon administration. Chapter 6 examines the favorable impact institutional factors associated with congressional decision-making processes had on Indian policy development in the 1970s. All of these factors are basic to understanding why Indian preferences were incorporated into the official policies of the seventies and how they continue to influence policy development outcomes.

A final note on the methodology employed in this study concludes this introduction (other references to method may be found in Appendix A). Briefly, my approach to the question, "How was Indian policy made in the seventies?" was three-pronged. Open-ended interviews were conducted with policy specialists (elites) who had been involved with Indian affairs during the seventies.[6] Legislative case studies were conducted on major legislation enacted between 1968 and 1980 (see Appendix B). Finally, the interviews with policy specialists were subjected to a computer-assisted content analysis.[7]

The period 1968 to 1980 was selected because the Indian takeover of Alcatraz Island marked the beginning of contemporary Indian political activism and the election of Ronald Reagan its end. The study has been updated to include references to the Reagan Indian Policy. It is left to the reader to decide if the shift to self-determination in Indian policy development reflects an enlightened approach that valorizes Indian control over Indian affairs, or whether it marks only a temporary aberration in the federal government's approach to legislating Indian affairs.

NOTES

1. The Merriam Report was commissioned by the federal government and published in 1928, the first of three such comprehensive studies on the negative impact of government policy on Indian development in the modern era. It extensively documented the material and economic underdevelopment of Indian communities, recommending that the government revise its policies in order to deal more effectively with problems of poverty, education, health, and economic development. The commission's findings influenced Indian policy

development during the progressive era of the 1930s, under Indian Commissioner John Collier's leadership. Also, in 1972 and in 1977, the Kennedy study on Indian education and the *Final Report* of the American Indian Policy Review Commission (AIPRC), under Senator Abourezk's leadership, were major government studies that documented substantially similar conditions and made similar recommendations. See *The Problem of Indian Administration*, a report of the survey made at the request of Honorable Hubert Work, Secretary of the Interior, and was submitted to him February 21, 1928, Lewis Merriam, Technical Director of Survey Staff (1928); U.S. Congress, Senate, Committee on Labor and Public Welfare, Special Subcommittee on Indian Education (1969), and AIPRC, *Report on Indian Education* (1976); see also, AIPRC, *Report on Alcohol and Drug Abuse* (1976, pp. 3–7); AIPRC, *Report on Indian Health* (1976, pp. 39–73); on the role of alcohol in Indian communities, and for a review of the literature on Indian alcohol abuse, see Klausner and Foulks (1982, pp. 5–8); Advance Reports, 1980 Census of Population and Housing (1981, pp. 4–10); Levitan and Johnston (1975, pp. 11–45); for an overview of federal programs available to Indians, see Jones (1982), and Taylor (1983, pp. 65–130).

2. For a description of public policy models see Dye (1981, pp. 19–45); and Woll (1974, pp. 21–52).

3. Two excellent summaries of the large literature describing the growth of interest groups and their meaning for American political processes and representation are Berry (1984, pp. 1–15); and Loomis and Cigler (1983, pp. 1–28).

4. On the importance of organizations for policy effectiveness, see Wilson (1973); Berry (1977); Walker (1983, pp. 390–406).

5. On this point, see Walker (1983, pp. 401–403).

6. I have used the term *elite* to identify those who have influence by being intimately involved with policy development processes (Dexter [1970, pp. 5–11]; Heclo's [1978, pp. 99–100, 105–115] definition of "specialist" is also appropriate).

7. The following references were helpful to me in choosing to proceed according to this methodology: Holsti (1969) and Krippendorff (1980).

1

The Failure of American Indian Policy: History's Verdict

American Indian studies are a mixed bag of scholarly accounts of the history of Indian-white relations, appeals to conscience, and journalistic and personal narratives about life as an Indian or life among the Indians. With few exceptions, these are not public policy studies (for example, Benham, 1977; Flood, 1980; Tyler, 1973; Taylor, 1983). Indian studies have been the province mainly of historians, anthropologists, and polemicists whose primary objective has been to chronicle the "Indian Experience" under white (non-Indian) domination or to record the transformations undergone by individual tribes due to contact with non-Indian systems (Washburn, 1974).

Despite the variety of academic perspectives involved, however, and with an impressive degree of consensus, these studies have documented the devastating impact of federal policy on the development of Indian tribes and communities. Indeed, a review of the literature on Indian-white relations makes it possible to conclude that there is general agreement that federal policy has had a predominantly negative impact on Indian populations. On the other hand, the literature does not tell us much about how Indian policy is made, to what extent Indian policy-making conforms to a theory of public policy development, or about the role Indians themselves may have played in making policy.

To date, the main contribution of Indian histories has been to establish that American Indians have been the victims rather than the beneficiaries or creators of federal Indian policy. Specifically with reference to its consequences, according to scholarly consensus, the history of Indian-white policy relations has been a failure. In contrast, this study presents evidence that Indian policy-making, at least during the 1970s, was a success in terms of achieving Indian policy preferences.

However, the question of failure or success is important to both historical and political analysis. Thus, a systematic approach to explaining how policy is formulated, which policy analysis provides and histories do not, is necessary for showing how democratic principles are extended to American minority populations and for determining how political constituencies may seek to influence policy decisions affecting their lives.

Furthermore, how democratic principles are extended to specific populations and interests gives us some idea of how we might reform policy processes to become even more representative of minority interests. By the same token, how political influence is obtained and exercised, and who are the key actors in this process, is knowledge that political constituencies may use to enhance the chance of having their interests protected by government. We may well ask, therefore, why more policy analyses have not been written.

It may be, as Francis Paul Prucha suggested, that Indian policy is viewed as anomalous, that is, as not fitting the frameworks for analysis generally applied to public policy studies.[1] This, then, is the idea that Indian-white policy relations arise out of peculiar circumstances, or in other words, that because of the trust relationship and the treaties, the Indian relationship is not like any other between government and a political constituency and therefore cannot be studied in the same way.

The view that Indian relations are unique in this sense is also reinforced by the belief that ethnic and racial minorities are oppressed and therefore democratic principles and institutions have failed them. Thus, colonial dependency theory, for example, explains Indian policy in Marxist or neo-Marxist terms (Johansen and Maestas, 1979; Jones, 1982; Jorgensen, 1972). This argument purports that American institutions, predicated as they are upon capitalism, must, by definition, exploit those who, like American Indians, are economically and politically powerless to defend their interests.

Another common form of interpretation views Indian policy as the product of manifest destiny. In other words, the intention and result of governmental policies has been to defraud the Indians of their land and natural resources, legally, or through the right of eminent domain.[2] Thus, historians focusing on the extent to which Indian populations have been defrauded of their lands imply a conspiracy theory of Indian affairs that has been the subject of extensive debate and the taking of sides.

Yet another reason for ignoring formal public policy studies of Indian affairs has to do with the low salience and visibility of Indian policy in general. Outside of those Indian populations and non-Indian constituencies directly affected by federal policy decisions, or those specialists who deal with Indian affairs in Congress on a regular basis, there is very little interest in the subject of Indian policy. Public policy analysts sensitive to establishing academic reputations are generally loath to pursue subjects that are unlikely to yield recognition because they are viewed as unimportant. Scholars who are unable to obtain financial support for the study of Indian policy are thus less likely to try. If we also take into account difficulties associated with Indian resistance to being studied, it is easier to understand why the subject of Indian policy has been neglected by academicians (Fellin, 1980; Garvin, 1976; *Journal of Social Issues*, 1977; Trimble, 1977).

Nevertheless, historians have tried to explain the political nature of Indian-white relations. In the process they have exposed the unconscionable ways in which society's promises to the Indian have been broken. Consequently, these studies have served to promote Indian interests by speaking to the moral conscience of America. In this endeavor, however, such analyses are notably bereft in suggesting how Indians and elected officials might practically go about achieving a more just and egalitarian relationship. Actually, studies that conclude that the present system does not work, fail to properly consider the alternative paradigm, that American Indian policy may work, or be made to work, just like any other product of democratic electoral and constitutional processes.

Thus, this study examines Indian policy development within the framework of constitutional and electoral systems. In doing so, it is found that the historical consensus on Indian policy as representing the failure of American democracy to protect and enhance minority interests does not adequately explain policy development since the 1970s. In order to understand contemporary Indian policy dynamics, however, we must first examine this historical consensus in greater detail. This purpose may be accomplished by designating three perspectives found in the historical literature: the conventional, the activist, and the minority group.

THE CONVENTIONAL TRADITION

The work of Francis Paul Prucha represents a classical approach to the writing of history (*Indian-White Relations*, 1982; Prucha, 1977;

United States Indian Policy, 1977). It is characterized as much by close, exhaustive attention to primary sources as by the effort to achieve balance and objectivity in the analysis. Even so, Prucha has been criticized for being too fair—for giving too much credit, that is, to the good intentions of policymakers in the past and attributing to them a genuine sense of justice in legislating Indian affairs (Washburn, 1977). Indeed, a common characteristic of Indian history writing is its preoccupation with blame (Blumenthal, 1955; Burnette, 1971; Coffer, 1979; Costo and Henry, 1977; Embry, 1956; Evarts, 1829; Gessner, 1931; Indian Rights Association, 1916; Jackson, 1964; Kinney, 1937; Leupp, 1910; McCreight, 1947; Nammack, 1969; Peithmann, 1964; Priest, 1942; Van Every, 1966). Although conventional historians usually attempt to adopt an objective, though sympathetic, stance toward their subjects, writing about Indian history has invariably meant taking sides, and Prucha was clearly on the side of the Indian.

With respect to the formative years of Indian policy, Prucha argued that the principles that would guide Indian policy-making—from the first Non-Intercourse Act of 1790 throughout most of the nineteenth century—were already in place by the end of the colonial era (Prucha, 1962). Thus, despite sustained opposition from the states, by the time of the First Continental Congress in 1775, it had become clear that Indian affairs was one area that would belong to the central government. As Prucha commented: "Whatever the ultimate source of congressional power, the federal government has never felt hampered for want of authority" (Prucha, 1962, p. 43).

Accordingly, early presidents and secretaries of war, Washington and Henry Knox in particular, "firmly established" the British practice of viewing the Indian tribes as independent sovereign nations (Prucha, 1962). It should also be noted that the principle of dealing with the tribes as sovereign nations, as evidenced by treaties negotiated with them until 1871, was a tradition established in the Congress of the United States rather than by the Supreme Court. In fact, the court, in decisions rendered in 1831 and 1832, established the contradictory principles that Indian nations were semisovereign or "domestic dependent nations" and that Congress had full plenary authority over them (Pevar, 1983).

More will be said about the ambivalent political status of Indian tribes in later chapters, because questions of political status are at the heart of policy debates on Indian affairs. For the moment, it will suffice to point out that the principle of congressional authority over Indian affairs was established early on.

Prucha (1962) also argued that presidents and politicians were mostly benevolent in their initiatives and were sometimes advocates of Indian rights. Their motivation—to keep Indians and whites separated on the frontier, in a conscious effort to avoid war and keep the peace—nevertheless backfired as the frontier was overrun with traders, speculators, and settlers eager to appropriate Indian lands for themselves, even when it meant ignoring official preferences.[3] The politicians did succeed, however, in enacting legislation intended to protect the Indians from white encroachments from the fur and whiskey trades and from unregulated settlement (Prucha, 1962). As might be expected from what we know about the difference between the intentions of policies and the way in which they are actually carried out, however, the well-meant laws of Washington policymakers fell far short of successfully establishing permanent boundaries for an "Indian country." Thus, although

the laws of Congress, the proclamations of the President, and the orders issued by the War Department did provide a brake on the westward-rolling juggernaut ... it cannot be denied that the land greed of the Whites forced the Indians westward ... behind the removal policy was the desire of eastern Whites for Indian lands and the wish for Indian states to be disencumbered of the embarrassment of independent groups of aborigines within their boundaries.[4]

Then, as now, the principle obstacle to protective Indian legislation was opposition from non-Indians: frontiersmen, traders, settlers, land developers, and the states themselves. Strikingly, the concept of an "Indian Country" remains a central issue in Indian affairs so that the bulk of Indian legislation today continues to deal with questions of land restoration and use, boundaries, jurisdictions, and claims.[5]

Prucha (1962) concluded that behind the failure of the official policies were diametrically opposed and irreconcilable notions about the character of the Indian people. Accordingly, whereas Washington policymakers themselves were inclined to view the Indian communities as sovereign entities, they were unable to change the popular conception of Indians as conquered savages, without sovereignty, and in need either of becoming assimilated or being annihilated in order to establish progress and civilization on the frontier.[6]

The difference in perspective between policymakers and the populations they represent is important. Differing views on the character and destiny of Indian peoples are still important dimensions of the policy debate, especially with respect to self-determination versus termination ideology. Furthermore, the durability of such views helps us to understand why, even after apparently successful legislative eras (as may have occurred in the 1930s and the 1970s) many analysts of Indian policy would nevertheless maintain that Indian policy is a failure.

THE ACTIVIST TRADITION

Historians writing in this tradition are not revisionist in the strictest sense. American historians have been critical of the federal government's actions in Indian relations from their earliest writings (Washburn, 1974). In contrast, the activist tradition in the writing of Indian history is perhaps best characterized by its forceful advocacy of what might broadly be termed "the Indian point of view." This bias is generally stated, with little pretense at objectivity or attempting to arrive at value-free judgment. Although we do not know who exactly in the Indian community is being spoken for, much of this writing is intensely preoccupied with exposing the exploitive nature of Indian-white relations and in documenting the wrongs perpetrated on Indian populations by nefarious governmental policies. Authors in this tradition concentrate on exposing abuses specifically with respect to land expropriations or Interior Department and Bureau of Indian Affairs (BIA) mismanagement and malfeasance (Brown, 1979; Cahn, 1969; McNickle, 1949; Steiner, 1968).

Perhaps better than anyone else writing as an activist, Vine Deloria, Jr.'s works exemplify their shared perspective: at the same time critical and condemnatory in their appraisal of past practices, yet sometimes hopeful about the direction future policies might take. Unlike most other writers in this tradition, however, Deloria is also a political scientist. As such, his work makes explicit reference to concepts that are useful for a political analysis of Indian affairs: its constitutional origins; the body of Indian law; social movement organizations; legislative policy dynamics; and, to the roles of Congress, the courts, and the executive in formulating and implementing Indian policy. Deloria, however, also makes it very clear that governmental institutions and processes have had a profoundly negative impact on the nature and operation of Indian tribal and other institutional structures. In addition, his early work, although more personal and anecdotal than the later books, is useful because it is based on his experiences as an Indian who has also been active in Indian politics for over twenty years, thus lending his arguments an immediacy and personal bias that helps us understand the climate of the times that prevailed in Indian policy-making circles during the late sixties and early seventies.

Besides his personal credentials, which have helped to establish him as an authority on Indian policy, Deloria's work is significant because it has been continuous. Between 1969 and 1985, for example, he published seven books on the subject of Indian affairs, along with numerous pieces in other publications (Deloria, 1969, 1970, 1971, 1973, 1974; Deloria and Lytle, 1983, 1984). Fortunately, the sheer volume of his work, much of which deals with the same themes but from different perspectives, enables us to identify what for Deloria and other activists have been the key issues in Indian-white relations; namely, treaty rights and obligations, the trust relationship, assimilation, termination, and self-determination policies and their impact on American Indian cultures and institutions. Like other activists, Deloria argued that Indian policy has failed to protect and enhance Indian interests by sacrificing them for those of non-Indian constituencies and the public interest.

Finally, Deloria and other activist writers are distinguished by their concern for reform. Deloria, for example, offered concrete proposals for making Indian nations politically sovereign, independent, political entities in the world system. Before proceeding to examine his proposals, a word about the preoccupation of Indian policy analysts with the concept of sovereignty is in order.

As can be shown for the contemporary case, the nature of Indian-white relations is complex and central to the debate on Indian sovereignty. As with other aspects of Indian policy, any attempt to understand the formal relationship that exists between the federal government and the tribes, or how it has changed over time, requires reference to hundreds of treaties, statutes, court decisions, and executive orders dating from the colonial era, as well as to theories, which like the doctrines of conquest, national sovereignty, or discovery, predate the establishment of the United States as a Republic. Fortunately, historians and others have grappled with the documentary data long enough that we are able to identify the more prominent themes and arguments that define the debate on Indian sovereignty.[7]

Deloria, like other analysts, makes reference to the commerce and treaty clauses of the Constitution that give Congress the power to regulate commerce with the states and with the Indian tribes. Thus, it has generally been agreed that the power to formulate Indian policy resides with Congress, if not in some absolutely philosophical sense, as Deloria argued, then at least legally (Deloria, 1983). Accordingly, Deloria argued: "Congressional policy should recognize the basic right to tribal sovereignty. Such sovereignty should include all premises contained in treaties and should recognize the eligibility of tribal governments for all federal programs which are opened to counties and cities" (Deloria, 1969, p. 144). In fact, lawyers in general take a similar point of view.[8] Without necessarily going so far as to argue for separate nation status, they nevertheless argue that Indians should be sovereign with respect to the exercise of jurisdictional powers that are an essential component of sovereignty (Medcalf, 1978). Thus, Indians should have the power to license, tax, zone, lease, and assume responsibility for economic development (Medcalf, 1978). As is pointed out in later chapters, how sovereignty is perceived by the various participants in the Indian policy arena significantly determines the policy approach Indians and their advocates, as well as their adversaries, will adopt.

Who shall have the authority for regulating Indian affairs is at the heart of most discussions of Indian policy because, at bottom, the question of Indian sovereignty is at stake. In the same way, much of the discussion about who should design Indian programs and who should operate them—themes common to policy development in the seventies—is a debate about in what ways and to what extent Indian tribes can be said to be self-governing, or sovereign. Deloria and others in the activist tradition, unlike those who represent official points of view, believe that sovereignty did not end for Indians with conquest and removal to the reservations.

Self-determination, Deloria (1984) argued, is an attribute of sovereign nations and, as such, Indian tribes and nations have always been self-determining. Thus, a major theme of Deloria's work is to show that Indians have never lost, nor given up, their sovereign status; in fact, "as tribes increasingly call themselves nations, partially in response to traditional arguments and partially as a means of emphasizing sovereignty against state and federal government, some form of national government must be devised" (p. 246).[9]

In support of these views, Deloria argued that it is because Indians perceive themselves as sovereign that they have resisted assimilation, fought termination, and preserved their cultures as much as possible. It is why the tribes have insisted, primarily through the courts, that the United States honor its treaty obligations (Deloria, 1984). To prove his point, Deloria reexamined judicial decisions beginning with the *Cherokee Nation v. Georgia* (1831), which are typically viewed as the prevailing interpretation of Indian status. Thus, he argued that Justice Marshall's definition of Indian tribes as "domestic dependent nations" (what the lawyers refer to as "quasi-sovereign") is not representative of the views court justices in general have held (Deloria, 1983; Medcalf, 1978).

Deloria's most distinctive contribution to the study of Indian-white relations, however, is his conclusion that the federal government must permit the tribes to constitute themselves as independent sovereign nations. Thus, in his most intriguing proposal, Deloria explained how separate nation status might be achieved. He argued that nation status cannot be denied on the basis of too small a population size or land base, or because the tribes may be land-locked communities, economically dependent, or educationally and administratively unsophisticated.[10] By contrast, he identified at least forty nations who also do not meet this criteria but are nevertheless sovereign, stating that Indian tribes can therefore be sovereign too.

Deloria's perception that the ongoing fundamental dilemma of Indian policy centers about the question of status is widely shared (Medcalf, 1978).[11] Nevertheless, official governmental positions on Indian political status—both tribal and federal—fall short of endorsing an absolute definition of sovereignty. It is against this background of competing views on the political status of Indian communities, that the findings of this study must be understood. Although my own objectives are more modest than to define Indian status, it will be impossible to understand respondents' views without reference to the sovereignty debate. Indian policy decisions significantly hinge on how Indian sovereignty is being defined by policymakers at any given point in time, regardless of what specific, substantive policy issue may be at stake. Thus, by explicitly or implicitly taking sovereignty as its central theme, the activist tradition goes to the heart of the matter and provides us with important insight into the centrality of sovereignty ideology for understanding Indian policy development.

AMERICAN INDIANS AS A MINORITY GROUP

Although not as clearly a separate tradition in the writing on Indian-white relations as either the conventional or the activist traditions just discussed, there has been some attempt in the literature to argue that Indians should be viewed as another minority group, or to show why this cannot be the case. The question is important not only because ethnicity and racial status are important variables for understanding the historical experience of racial minorities in American society—and therefore the nature of their participation, or lack of it, in American political institutions and processes—but also because the minority status designation is useful for understanding the motivation behind federal policy actions since the mid 1960s.[12]

Thus, analysts, like Alvin Josephy, Jr., and Stan Steiner, have chosen to study the "Red Power" movement, suggesting that Indian militancy and activism are social movements analogous to those of blacks and Hispanics (Josephy, 1972; Steiner, 1968). Others, like Murray Wax, adopted a more traditional assimilationist perspective, arguing that Indians, like other minorities, will eventually enter the mainstream of American society (Eggan, 1966; Wax, 1971; Yinger and Simpson, 1978). Yet other analysts, such as Sar Levitan and Edgar Cahn, pointed out how Indians benefit from, or are exploited by, federal social welfare programs aimed at meeting the special needs of Indians and other minorities (Levitan and Johnston, 1975; Taylor, 1983).[13]

The view that Indians are a minority group, like blacks, Hispanics, or any other American racial minority, has been useful for policy development. This was especially so during the late 1960s and early 1970s when so much money was available to be spent exclusively on programs for minority populations. Nevertheless, other analysts reject the comparison, pointing out that Indians are not only a culturally distinct population but also that their prior claim on the North American continent sets them apart from all other groups. Thus, we have Deloria's widely accepted contention, for example, that the basic difference between blacks and Indians is that the former are pursuing equality of acceptance as well as of opportunity in American society, whereas the latter are pursuing justice (Deloria, 1969, 1974; Medcalf, 1978). By justice Deloria meant the right to preserve a separate political autonomy and cultural identity as well as to benefit from policies aimed at compensating the Indian for past wrongs. All of these goals are represented in the Indian preoccupation with claiming sovereignty and maintaining a separate land base and are thus different from those of other American minorities.

These distinctions between justice and equality in the minority groups' literature are also important because they explain why the views of Indians and government officials often differ. The predisposition of Indians and their advocates is to view the ultimate objective of Indian policy as the preservation of Indian autonomy and the land base. The disposition of government officials—elected or appointed— has been to view their dealings with the Indian in the same light as with any disadvantaged population, that is, in terms of extending benefits, opportunities, and social equality to those who are poor. Obviously, the pursuit of land-related policy objectives will differ from the pursuit of egalitarian social welfare policies. Generally, each type of policy involves different actors in policy negotiations and may elicit varying levels of support, although, during the 1970s, Indians made significant gains in both policy areas.

For many analysts, therefore, the differences in Indian and non-Indian perspectives on the question of minority rights are fundamental to understanding why Indians have fared so poorly at the hands of government. At the heart of this difference in perspective is how each defines "Indian." Thus, we may contrast Deloria's views, or those of Frances Svensson, to those of non-Indian policymakers. For example, Deloria (1984) said:

When we understand the idea of the people, we can also learn how the idea of the treaty became so sacred to Indians that even today, more than a century after most of the treaties were made, Indians still refer to the provisions as if the agreement were made last week.... The idea of "the people"... with most American Indian tribes... begins somewhere in the primordial mists. (p. 8)

This notion of their own uniqueness also helps to explain Svensson's definition of Indian: "At its heart, Indianness is a state of being, a cast of mind, a relationship to the universe. It is undefinable" (Svensson, 1973, p. 9).[14]

Unlike Indian analysts, however, policymakers have settled for a much more prosaic definition of Indian. For the purposes of allocating resources and determining who shall be eligible to benefit, policymakers have thus operationalized Indian to mean the tribe's own definition, that of the BIA, which emphasizes blood quanta, or that of the Census Bureau, which permits self-identification.[15] Obviously, these profoundly differing notions of who or what is Indian enable us to see that sometimes irreconcilable differences are encountered when setting policy goals. As the findings on policymakers' ideas about Indian sovereignty and self-determination put forth in this study will suggest, varying notions about who or what is Indian make for confusion and dissension in the arena of Indian policy-making.

THE SPECIAL NATURE OF INDIAN HISTORY

As is evident from this examination of approaches to the study of Indian history, scholars have focused almost entirely on the negative impact of federal policy for the development of Indian communities. Specifically, they have attributed poverty, the erosion of sovereignty, the undermining of cultural integrity, and the loss of a land base to federal policies that have been intended both to assimilate Indian populations to mainstream Anglo-Saxon norms and to achieve the imperatives of manifest destiny. Nothing more effectively illustrates this point, perhaps, than a partial sampling of book titles (in chronological order): *Essays on the Present Crisis in the Condition of the American Indians* (Evarts, 1829), *The Indian and His Problem* (Leupp, 1910), *Vicious Indian Legislation: A Brief Analysis of Bills Now Pending in Congress That Ought to be Defeated* (Indian Rights Association, 1916), *Massacre: A Survey of Today's American Indian* (Gessner, 1931), *A Continent Lost—A Civilization Won: Indian Land Tenure in America* (Kinney, 1937), *Uncle Sam's Stepchildren: The Reformation of U.S. Indian Policy, 1885–1887* (Priest, 1942), *Firewater and Forked Tongues: A Sioux Chief Interprets U.S. History* (McCreight, 1947), *American Indians Dispossessed: Fraud in Land Cessions Forced Upon the Tribes* (Blumenthal, 1955), *America's Concentration Camps: The Facts About Our Indian Reservations Today* (Embry, 1956), *A Century of Dishonor: A Sketch of the United States Government's Dealings with Some of the Indian Tribes* (Jackson, 1964), *Broken Peace Pipes: A Four Hundred Year History of the American Indian* (Peithmann, 1964), *Disinherited: The Lost Birthright of the American Indian* (Every, 1966), *Fraud, Politics and the Dispossession of the Indians* (Nammack, 1969), *The Tortured Americans* (Burnette, 1971), *Indian Treaties: Two Centuries of Dishonor* (Costo and Henry, 1977), *Phoenix: The Decline and Rebirth of the Indian People* (Coffer, 1979).

In the end, the historical record of the failure of federal Indian policy serves in contradistinction to the findings of the present study. Although there can be little argument that federal policy has failed to improve the quality of life in Indian populations, or to be predictably trustworthy in protecting Indian rights, it can be shown that Indian political entities significantly enhanced their ability to influence the development of federal policies favorable to their own goals after 1970.

The shift that took place in Congress' approach to Indian policy development, away from termination and toward self-determination, is revealed in major legislation enacted during the 1970s: for example, the Alaska Native Claims Settlement Act of 1971, the Indian Education Act of 1972, the Menominee Restoration Act of 1973, the Indian Self-Determination and Educational Assistance Act of 1975, the Indian Health Care Improvement Act of 1976, the Indian Child Welfare Act of 1978, and the Maine Indians Claims Settlement Act of 1980 (see Appendix B for a complete list). The policy dynamics—arguments for and against decision-making processes, and the actions of interested publics associated with the formulation and enactment of this legislation—present a clear picture of how a value for Indian self-determination has become the central principle of contemporary Indian policy-making. The following chapters explain how this shift in the orientation of Congress toward Indian affairs occurred and how Indians themselves were instrumental in bringing it about. We begin with the finding that the oldest of the policy-making principles involved in the legislation of Indian affairs—the constitutional mandate—is still very much alive.

NOTES

1. Prucha (1962) quoted Lewis Cass (1830) and Justice John Marshall (1831), respectively, to this effect: "The Indians themselves are an anomaly upon the face of the earth; and the relations, which have been established between them and the nations of Christendom, are equally anomalous. Their intercourse is regulated by practical principles, arising out of peculiar circumstances"; "the condition of the Indians in relation to the United States is perhaps unlike that of any other two people in existence" (p. 1).

2. Most Activist analyses are of this type. See Cahn (1969, 1970) on abuses of the BIA; Kickingbird and Ducheneaux (1973) for examples of abuse with reference to land sales and claims; Josephy (1984) for an explanation of how Indians continue to have to battle racial stereotypes, for retaining their spirituality, for their land, water, hunting, and fishing rights and for self-determination (Steiner, 1968).

3. Prucha (1962, pp. 44–64) and Horsman (1971, 1981) argued that peace was preferable to war because war was perceived as too costly an alternative.

4. Prucha (1982, pp. 147, 224) and Horsman (1981) added that "wholesale

land acquisition *and* [my italics] friendship with the Indians were incompatible" (p. 96).

5. "Indian Country" remains an important concept in today's Indian policies. Generally, the concept refers to any location—spatial or temporal, attitudinal or geographic—where Indians reside. Legally, the technical definition, in effect since 1948, is as follows:

(a) all land within the limits of any Indian reservation under the jurisdiction of the United States government, notwithstanding the issuance of any patent, and, including rights-of-way running through the reservation; (b) all dependent Indian communities within the borders [sic] of the United States whether within the original or subsequently acquired territory thereof, and whether within or without the limits of a state, and, i.e., all Indian allotments, the Indian titles to which have not been extinguished. (Cohen, 1982, p. 27)

6. This conclusion is a major theme of Prucha's analysis and can be clearly seen in the contrast between Presidents Washington and Jefferson's views to those of President Andrew Jackson, which Prucha (1962, p. 213) provides (see also, Berkohofer, 1978, 1979, pp. 25ff).

7. Two of the earliest and most enduring definitions are those of Chief Justice John Marshall in the *Cherokee Nation v. Georgia* (30 U.S. [5 Pet.] 1 [1831]) and Cohen (1942); see also, the American Indian Policy Review Commission, *Final Report*, 1977. Former Congressman Lloyd Meed's views on sovereignty in this report are in contrast to those of Deloria and the activists.

8. In Cohen's (1942) book, for example, we find the following statement: "Perhaps the most basic principle of all Indian law...is the principle that those powers which are lawfully invested in an Indian tribe are not, in general, delegated powers granted by express acts of Congress, but rather inherent powers of a limited sovereignty which has never been extinguished" (p. 122).

9. John Echohawk, of the Native American Rights Fund, stated a similar sentiment: "More and more people are coming to accept the proposition that Indian tribes should regain their place alongside the federal and state governments as independent units...the fear, or the hope, that the tribes will have their special status and very existence terminated by Washington and just fade away is gone now" (Knight, 1979).

10. For a detailed argument on each of these points, see Deloria (1974, pp. 161–176). Also note that the subtitle to *Trail* is "an Indian Declaration of Independence." Deloria intended to convey the message that he means "independence" (separate national status) by "sovereignty."

11. In addition, Felix Cohen eloquently illustrated how long it is that the question of sovereignty has plagued Indian Affairs:

In the history of western thought, theologians, missionaries, judges, and legislators for 400 years and more have consistently recognized the right of Indians to manage their own affairs. Nothing that we could say today in defense of Indian rights of self-government could be as eloquent as the works of Francisco de Vitoria in 1532 or of Pope Paul III in 1537 or Bartholomew de Las Casas in 1542 or of Chief Justice John Marshall in 1832. For 400 years, men who have looked at the matter without the distortions of material prejudice or bureaucratic power have seen that the safety and freedom of all of us is inevitably tied up with the safety and freedom of the weakest and tiniest of our minorities. This is not novel vision but ancient wisdom. What gives point to the problem in 1949 is that after 422 years of support for the principle of Indian self-government there is so little Indian self-government. (Josephy, 1971, 1972, p. 19)

12. Two attempts to address questions of Indian political participation are Rader (1978) and Ritt (1979, pp. 45–72).

13. Cahn (1969, 1970) is especially keen in pointing out how the BIA has mismanaged Indian programs.

14. Other definitions of Indian refer to specific cultural characteristics or social traits. For example, Wax [(1971, p. 4)]; Spicer (1982) defined them as "a number of people who share a particular Indian group name and other symbols of a common historical experience unique to those who share the group name" (p. 16).

15. There is quite a debate on the issue of defining Indian (Ayres, 1978, pp. 22–27; Bounpane, 1983, pp. 1–8). For an explanation of why Indians reject the operational definitions see, for example, the definition of Indian found in the Indian Education Act (PL 92–318) (Henry and Costo, 1980, pp. 15–18).

2

The Constitutional Mandate on Indian Affairs and the Role of Law

In their discussion of the factors that contribute most significantly to the development of federal Indian policy, policy specialists frequently cite the role played by treaties and the courts in determining what shall be the intent and substance of new legislation (see Table 2.1). In turn, the part played by treaties and the courts in Indian policy development reflects what may be termed the federal government's constitutional mandate or obligation to legislate Indian affairs in accordance with the principles of the trust relationship.

The trust relationship is difficult to define. Thus, although policymakers have relied very heavily on judicial interpretation, existing statute, and the terms of treaties and executive orders in deciding what will be legislated and to what ends, they have also sought to do the right thing with respect to defining the trust relationship at any given time. Therefore, in the view of policy specialists, the mandate to legislate Indian affairs is as much a state of mind or moral attitude as it is a complex body of Indian law stemming from Congress' constitutional authority to regulate Indian affairs.[1]

The observation that the constitutional mandate on Indian affairs is ideology as well as moral and legal principle is essential for understanding how Indians came to exert influence on policy development

Table 2.1
Sources of Legal and Statutory Influence on Indian Policy
Development

Source	Percent of Respondents Citing Source[a]	Number of Times Mentioned in an Interview[b]	
		1 and 2	3 or More
Courts	59.1	40	51
Treaties	47.0	24	25

[a]The percentage cited refers only to those respondents who mentioned a particular source of influence in the interview. Thus, of a possible sixty-six respondents who might have referred to courts as important, thirty-nine, or 59.1 percent of them, actually cited courts as a source of influence worth mentioning. This means that twenty-seven respondents did not mention courts. For these reasons, percentages do not total 100.

[b]The number of mentions is meant to provide some indication of the intensity or importance with which the respondent viewed the source cited. Thus, for example, courts are perhaps an even more basic influence on policy development because they are mentioned nearly twice as many times as treaties; thirty-nine respondents mentioned courts a total of ninety-one times.

during the 1970s. Unfortunately, however, ideological and moral considerations are not weighed very heavily in policy analysis. Thus, scholars often disregard the significance of values and beliefs for understanding how official decisions are made. Nevertheless, Indian policy development during the 1970s clearly would not have taken the shape it did without the support of public officials who believed Indians had been treated unjustly in this sense. One policy specialist put the common view as follows:

It was a long time ago, but I think the movement to pass Indian legislation has been there since the birth of the Republic and our obligations to the Indian. In the sixties and seventies it was an outgrowth of the Great society push to lift the poor out of poverty and bring the downtrodden along. In 1946, the Indian Claims Commission was set up and there was an effort then to do something which went on through... Nixon's time. Indians were seen as politically appropriate. There was a lot of symbolism mixed into it—to see who could do how much for the Indians... but there was also a genuine hope for bettering the lives of Indians... that was real, people were dedicated, symbolism aside, to the principle of self-determination.*

The ideological orientations of policymakers have obviously, however, also been detrimental to the pursuit of Indian constituency policy goals and preferences. Senator Arthur Watkins and his colleagues in the 83rd Congress, for example, were as firm in their belief that Indian reservations ought to be dissolved as Senator Jim Abourezk, in the 93rd Congress, twenty years later, was sure they should be recognized or restored. Watkins, of course, believed that Indians would be better off if they assimilated—became more like other Americans. Abourezk, on the other hand, believed that Indians had a sovereign right to decide their own destinies. At the same time, there can be no doubt that Senator Watkins' belief was instrumental in creating termination policy or that Senator Abourezk's was decisive in bringing about that of self-determination.

In addition to how the mandate has been historically defined, the variable nature of Indian affairs can thus be explained by certain legal, moral, and ideological tensions that are inherent in the constitutional mandate. These tensions, and the contradictory ways in which they are resolved from one policy epoch to another, are what give Indian policy its cyclical appearance. One result of these dynamics has been to view Indian affairs legislation as a study in failure. Another result has been to see Indian policy as entirely dependent on the whims of political administrations and the courts. In either case, Indian policy

_____

*These are anonymous respondent views and they appear throughout the book.

development is seen as random occurrence, rather than as the result of institutionalized, and predictable, decision-making processes.

For these reasons, recognizing the existence of certain ever-present tensions in Indian policy development enables a much more systematic analysis of Indian policy formulation than has been the case. Thus, the question of how the Indians' political status will be defined is, implicitly or explicitly, a part of Indian policy discussions. Whether Indians are to be more or less sovereign is thus a permanent consideration when legislating Indian affairs. In addition, the Congress is always concerned with how questions of public and private interest will be resolved. At issue here is balancing the oftentimes conflicting interests of Indian and non-Indian constituencies. Moreover, how the trust relationship is being defined is predictably influential in developing a position on Indian affairs legislation. Thus, whether the Congress acts to forcefully advocate for the rights of Indians, or not, will significantly influence policy outcomes. In view of the fact that these tensions are perennial to Indian policy debates, policy specialists report that they importantly influenced the decisions made in the 1970s.

Given the existence of these tensions in Indian policy development, and the fact that they have defied attempts to definitely resolve the underlying questions at stake, Indian legislation is often contradictory or seems to reverse itself. Consequently, during the policy-making epoch that began with Richard Nixon's election to the presidency, in 1968, and continues in the present, the trust relationship was redefined to mean advocacy for greater Indian control over their internal affairs, mostly by expanding the role of Indians in decision-making processes and program development. By the same token, the question of political status was resolved in favor of greater self-determination for Indian tribes and communities and, thus, away from the terminationist orientation of earlier eras. And the tension between Indian and non-Indian interests was moderated by the emergence of a value for legislative over litigative solutions, which consistently favored Indian policy preferences.

These, then, constituted the operative policy-making principles of the seventies. Two of them—the value for self-determination and the preference for legislation over litigation—are examined in this chapter. The third—the value for advocacy—is examined in the discussion of congressional influence on Indian policy development.

SELF-DETERMINATION AS A POLICY-MAKING PRINCIPLE: SOLVING THE PROBLEMS CREATED BY PAST POLICIES

Elected officials adopted a self-determination ideology as an operative policy-making principle during the seventies, and this was an important dimension of the shift toward a pro-Indian perspective on Indian affairs. At the same time, their view of self-determination meant acting in keeping with a much stricter, or narrower, definition of the trust relationship than had previously been true. Thus, the Congress' drift toward indiscriminately exercising the plenary, near absolute, powers it had been granted in 1903 (*Long Wolf v. Hitchcock*) was reversed (for example, Hall, 1979; Pevar, 1983).

Thus, self-determination, after 1970, came to mean interpreting the trusteeship as protecting and enhancing the well-being of Indians, even when this approach meant trading off non-Indian interests. Accordingly, this new view of self-determination also implied that, at least for the decade of the seventies, the tension associated with ambivalence in defining the trust relationship would be resolved in favor of Indian preferences. This development in the Congress had its counterpart in the Supreme Court's "canons of treaty construction," which expressed a value for deciding treaty uncertainties in favor of what the Indians' understanding might have been (Pevar, 1983). Importantly, adopting the value for self-determination was a liberal shift in the Congress' approach to Indian policy development. At the same time, however, it also meant adhering more strictly to the federal government's role as trustee than had been the case for quite some time.

Ideological shifts by themselves, despite being a necessary condition for understanding Indian policy development, are nevertheless insufficient for bringing about fundamental changes in American policymaking processes, which are far more pragmatic than ideological in orientation. Thus, self-determination was a useful policy-making principle because the need to solve the policy problems and dilemmas created by past policy decisions had become politically urgent.

Policy specialists were emphatic in their views that the society of the times' value for civil rights for minorities required the federal government to try to rectify historic injustices. Political action was therefore prudent and feasible. Three problem-solution relationships serve to illustrate this argument: (a) the problem created by the Dawes Allotment policy of 1887 and the solution to it proposed by the Indian Reorganization Act (IRA) of 1934; (b) the problem created by termination policy (HCR 108 and PL 280), formalized in 1953, and the solution to it proposed by the Indian Self-Determination and Educational Assistance Act of 1975; and (c) the problem created by the violation of treaty rights by the federal government—in particular land expropriations—and the proposed solutions to this problem represented by the Land Claims Act of 1946 and restoration and recognition legislation. Each of these cases illustrates how self-determination ideology worked to legislate solutions to problems that had been created for the Indians by the federal government.

The Dawes, or General Allotment Act of 1887, was rationalized in the name of assimilating the Indian to mainstream cultural values of the time—namely, to the individual ownership of property, and the adoption of economically self-sufficient life-styles, as in farming and ranching. The idea was to free Indians to become civilized by taking away communally or tribally owned property and replacing it with individual ownership—in other words, to sever the reservations into allotments that could be owned and disposed of by individuals and families.

Other legislation, in 1902 and 1907, made the sale of Indian lands to non-Indians possible (Jackson and Galli, 1977). Allotment created problems of fractionated heirship and tribal land losses, problems that reorganization legislation, after 1934, and self-determination legislation, after 1975, were intended to resolve.[2] In effect, these land losses reduced the area of Indian reservations from 130,730,190 acres to 43,035,734, for a total loss of 87,623,456, or two-thirds of original reservation lands, by the time allotment legislation was rescinded in 1934 (Jackson and Galli, 1977; Officer, 1971).

Thus, what the allotment legislation actually accomplished was to facilitate the sale of Indian lands to speculators, developers, and other non-Indians and to leave many Indians homeless, without the means either to make a living or to retain their tribal identity. The rhetoric that had accompanied allotment legislation served to obscure the problem that Indians had become even more impoverished and destitute under allotment than they had been prior to it.

The fact that Indians were materially worse off, their cultures critically eroded, and that they remained unassimilated led to action. It was left to the Indian Reorganization Act of 1934 to formally end the practice of allotment that had been so harmful to the tribes. The act did so in the name of acknowledging the Indians' right to a separate cultural and political identity. Importantly, the act also provided a mechanism for establishing tribal self-government on the reservations. Although the latter accomplishment has been criticized as seriously flawed because the tribes were asked to model their constitutions after that of the United States, thus oftentimes violating their own cultural norms and practices, the IRA did serve as a foot-in-the-door for later claims to Indian sovereignty and self-determination.[3] Thus, the Indian Self-Determination and Educational Assistance Act of 1975, for example, attempted to extend the principle of Indian self-government by permitting the tribes to choose to administer their own services and programs through contracts negotiated with the Secretaries of Interior and Health and Human Services, among others, and in lieu of having these services administered by the Bureau of Indian Affairs (BIA).

Other legislation, much of it developed during the 1970s, also attempted to extend greater decision-making power and control over their resources to the tribes. Thus, the Indian Land Consolidation Act of 1983 addressed the problem of fractionated heirships. The Maine and Alaska settlements, of course, restored large tracts of land to Indian control. Furthermore, the Indian Mineral Development Act (1982) permitted tribes desiring to do so to enter into joint venture agreements with companies wanting to engage in energy development projects on the reservations. Along different lines, the Indian Tax Status Act (1983) allowed the tribes to issue revenue and development bonds, also a prerogative of politically sovereign entities.

Although self-determination legislation like this has the potential to enhance Indian self-governance and add to the land base, there can be little question that, to date, it has been intended to do so within the existing constitutional framework. In other words, Congress' plenary authority in relation to tribal matters remains intact and, as yet, Indian governments cannot choose to establish separate political structures for the definition and pursuit of their own goals.

There are other considerations that constrain the ability of Indians to exercise greater autonomy in managing their affairs. Chief among these is the reality that economic and social development requires resources that the poorer tribes lack. For example, it takes money, expertise, and experience to capitalize on the natural resources that some tribes have. The vast majority of tribes are poor in this sense. Thus, the absence of these resources makes it difficult, if not impossible, for many tribes to take advantage of the opportunities self-determination legislation makes available. This is the reason that such legislation is often accompanied by provisions that also make certain funds or technical assistance available to tribes and Indian communities desirous of exercising their right to manage their own development.

Moreover, it remains possible for tribes exercising greater autonomy in decision making to make decisions that may have unanticipated consequences detrimental to long-term tribal interests, like unwise economic investments or the erosion of tribal identity. Nevertheless, as these examples illustrate, legislation enacted in 1934 and during the 1970s points to two conclusions. First, that the 1934 legislation was a response to the problems created by allotment. Second, we can see that self-determination legislation is intended to solve problems caused by the federal government's inclination to impose control over how Indians should govern themselves and decide their internal affairs.

Another set of problems was created by House Concurrent Resolution 108 (HR 108) and PL 83–280 (PL 280), passed in 1953. Popularly known as "termination policy," although never formally enacted as such, these statutes were also rationalized as a means to free the Indian from federal responsibility by unilaterally ending the trust relationship with certain selected tribes. Between 1954 and 1956, therefore, Congress chose to terminate more than 100 tribes, among the largest of which were the Klamath in Oregon and the Menominee in Wisconsin (Pevar, 1983; Tyler, n.d.). These actions meant that treaties or other formal agreements with the tribes were abrogated or nullified, and that services and other rights extended to the tribes via the trust relationship were ended. It also meant, in most cases, that former tribal societies would become subject to the laws of the states—either as counties, as with the Menominees, or as individuals.

The relocation programs, which were implemented at the same time, had as their goal enabling Indians to leave the reservations, usually for urban environments. There, it was reasoned, they would find employment and the prosperity and assimilation that had eluded them on the reservations (Nagata, 1971; Sorkin, 1978; Svensson, 1973). As with the push to dissolve the reservations, the rhetoric accompanying relocation programs emphasized greater freedom and self-sufficiency for Indians by forcing them away from dependence on federal programs and by breaking the tie to federal paternalism in Indian affairs. These were ideals to which many Indians as well as non-Indians could subscribe. The forcefulness with which they were advocated by proponents, like Senator Arthur Watkins, served to gloss over or obscure the very real problems and material consequences that befell those tribes affected by termination and relocation policies.

Termination and the relocation policy proved a disaster.[4] Indians whose reservations had been dissolved, or who had relocated, not only failed to prosper but their material and economic circumstances worsened to the point of acute poverty. By 1973, when hearings were held on the question of restoring the Menominee lands to reservations status, the problems created by termination had grown too large to ignore. In fact, the arguments that proved most persuasive to Congress in deciding to restore the Menominee to tribal status, as per tribal wishes, revolved around the tribe's poverty and the cost to state and federal governments (Lurie, 1972; Orfield, 1965). As one respondent observed: "The Menominee restoration effort was the product of good leadership. They saw termination as tremendous disaster and even though no tribe had ever reversed termination, this was an era when people said, 'Let's go ahead and try it anyway.'" As Senator William Proxmire (D-Wisconsin) put it at the time: "Since 1961 [when the reservation was terminated], it has cost the American taxpayer over $19 million to support a tribe that before termination was able to pay for its own support" (Hearings, House Subcommittee on Indian Affairs, 1973).

The problems caused by termination, both with respect to the subsequent poverty and social dissolution of the tribes, as well as with respect to violations of the constitutional mandate on Indian affairs, are well-documented and, among other things, led to the Menominee Restoration Act (Peroff, 1982). Policy specialists clearly understand, however, that as much as self-determination has helped to solve problems created by past policies, Indian constituencies continue to regard it with suspicion, not trusting that another termination era may not be just around the corner. Nevertheless, respondents view Indian opposition to termination and the problems associated with it as having been primarily responsible for Congress' decision to restore the reservations to its former status.

The profound reaction to termination . . . stirred Indian Country from one end to the other. They were deeply fearful of termination and this stimulated pan-Indianism and organizations like the NCAI [National Congress of American Indians]. . . . It [termination] moved Indians out of their apathy and set the stage for . . . an enormous spurt of growth . . . which combined with a growing militancy as a by-product of the civil rights era, and, they began to enjoy important court victories. . . . So, gradually there has been an accretion of law to build tribal law into federal law so that there are three units of government—state, federal, and tribal. One result of this is that it makes it unlikely that we can turn the clock back to the days of termination . . . note the Reagan Administration "government to government" doctrine . . . they [Indians] are participants in and not the objects of policymaking.

That other reservations dissolved under termination have also been restored because of the Menominee, and other tribes recognized under federal statute for the first time, is further evidence of the ability of individual Indian entrepreneurs, like Ada Deer, and Indian organizations, like DRUMS (Determination of Rights and Unity for Menominee Shareholders), to lobby successfully for their policy goals. In the process, they helped to solve major problems stemming from termination.

TREATY RIGHTS AND THE INDIAN CLAIMS COMMISSION: ESTABLISHING A VALUE FOR LEGISLATIVE OVER LITIGATIVE STRATEGIES

Much, if not most, Indian policy legislation is concerned with treaty rights. In these matters, the approximately 650 treaties (nearly every tribe has one) that were negotiated or ratified between 1778 and 1871, when the Congress ended the practice of treaty making with the Indians, by means of a rider attached to the Indian Appropriations Act of March 3, 1871 (Sec. 2079), have proved to be the major source of disputation between the federal government and the Indians.[5] The bulk of these disputes center around problems involving the loss of Indian lands. In fact, the federal government's notoriety in refusing to honor the terms of the treaties—whether through fraud, mismanagement, or abrogation—has been the main subject not only of scholarly studies but of film and literature as well.[6]

The inclination of state and federal governments to ignore treaty rights and boundaries, and the desire of private interests to encroach on Indian territories for personal gain have resulted in innumerable instances of treaty violation. Despite enormous odds, the tribes have nevertheless sought to resist these actions, typically, by going to court. The federal government, as a sovereign, of course, is immune to suit except as it permits suit to be brought against itself. Thus, between 1863, when Congress barred any claims arising from Indian treaties, and 1946, when Congress passed the Indian Claims Settlement Act, the only way the tribes could bring suit in the Court of Claims was through the enactment of special statutes permitting certain tribes to sue. The tribes first had to obtain the legislation and then go through litigation before a claim could be settled. Although 185 cases were brought in this manner, fewer than 30 percent resulted in judgments to the Indians (United Effort Trust, n.d.).

The decisions of the Claims Court, established in conjunction with the Land Claims Act of 1946, however, contributed significantly to the momentum for pro-Indian policy change. Between 1946 and 1978, when the Claims Court ceased to operate (later Indian claims were referred to the U.S. Court of Claims), most of the Claims Court's monetary awards went to provide recourse for treaty-related grievances by enabling the tribes to file suit in such cases. The tribes did just that—in such large numbers that the commission had to be extended by legislation several times before it lapsed in 1978. These events were much to the chronic chagrin of those members of Congress who may have originally thought that the Claims Court, by finding against the tribes, might serve to end Indian claims forever.

There are two other noteworthy consequences of the era of the Claims Court. First, the litigation of Indian land rights emerged as a source of big money for lawyers and law firms willing to take the risk. One respondent observed in this respect: "Ten percent of ten million is an incentive." This trend implies that the tribes began to take advantage of expertise previously unavailable to them and to succeed more often in winning their cases. Second, Indian constituencies and interest groups were provided with an additional channel through which to exercise the advantages of their special access to governmental policy processes.

Importantly, land claims monetary and land settlements are an expression of the federal government's acknowledgment of the sovereignty of Indian tribes—their right to a land base—which is an inherent principle of the constitutional mandate on Indian affairs. They are also an example of the preference for legislation over litigation, which is another of the operative policy-making principles that emerged from the realm of Indian policy in the 1970s. A brief description of the Alaska and Maine cases serves to further illustrate this argument.

The Alaska and Maine land claims settlements, although there have been other smaller successes as well, were the examples most often cited by policy specialists in talking about the preference for legislation over litigation. Both of these settlements arose out of historical disputes over who owned the land.

In the Alaska case, native constituencies prepared the way for legislation, first in 1951, by filing claims with the Indian Claims Commission, and then, by filing protests against land selections that were to be made by the state of Alaska after statehood. Natives protested on the basis of the Organic Act of 1884 and the Statehood Act of 1958 that contained specific clauses vaguely protecting native rights. By 1968, forty protests covering 296,600,000 acres had been lodged with the Bureau of Land Management (Senate Report No. 92–405, 1971).

Despite these protests, in September 1966, large blocks of land on the north slope of the Brooks Range were opened for oil and gas exploration. Again, native groups protested, and three months later Secretary of Interior Stewart Udall froze leasing until native objections had been dealt with. These events enabled natives to "cloud title" to the land—to prevent use or development until questions of Indian ownership were resolved. It thus became impossible for the state of Alaska to proceed with land selections or for non-Indian oil interests to proceed with development of the Alaska pipeline (Berry, 1975).

So effective were native protests and the freeze, that in the 1969 Senate confirmation hearings on the appointment of Walter Hickel to be Secretary of Interior, Interior Committee chairman, Henry Jackson, was able to obtain a promise from the former governor of Alaska that he would pursue a settlement of the native claims. Similarly, respondents comment that presidential assistant John Erlichman is supposed to have applied pressure in order to obtain Secretary of Interior Rogers Morton's compliance with the Nixon administration's pro-settlement position, which was much more generous than that originally proposed by the Senate.[7]

Settlement legislation was developed between 1966 and December 1971, when the Alaska Native Claims Settlement Act (ANCSA) was enacted—leaving 40 million acres and $962.5 million to be distributed among and managed by native regional corporations. Native lobbies were so prominent during this time—much of the negotiation revolved around native claims to 60 million acres and the final compromise—

that respondents still remember seeing native Alaskans waiting in congressmen's offices wearing mukluks—the colorful footgear for which Eskimos are known—in July weather.

The Alaska settlement was unprecedented in its size and clearly illustrates the degree to which Indian claims were taken seriously. It also unequivocally illustrates the value for legislating Indian claims rather than permitting them to languish in the courts, thereby holding up attending to the concerns of non-Indian public and private interests. In fact, Indian interests then, as now, have used the strategy of "clouding the title" very effectively to get action on land claims issues. The Senate Committee on Interior and Insular Affairs speaks pointedly to the value for legislation over litigation in its final report.

This Committee believes that doing justice to Alaska's Native people and acting on the larger national interest both demand a prompt settlement on these claims. Their unresolved status threatens Native livelihoods and opportunities, the fiscal and economic viability of the state of Alaska and the proper conservation and development of Alaska's resources. Moreover, the Committee is convinced that the urgency and complexity of these issues, the need for statewide joint federal-state land use planning, and the necessity of reviewing all public lands in Alaska to determine which areas should be made a part of the National Park, National Forest, and National Wildlife Refuge Systems—especially the urgency of the Natives' need for better living conditions—*requires the certainty, the flexibility and the detail of a legislative settlement rather than a judicial settlement* [my italics]. This is a position shared by all of the parties involved—the Native people, the state of Alaska, the Administration, the Nation's major conservation organizations, and the Committee. (Senate Report No. 92–204, 1971, p. 62)

The Alaska Settlement was not easily arrived at and its story is still not over. Nevertheless, the views expressed by then Congressman John H. Kyl (R-Iowa), who had been a member of the committee, have prevailed: "If we adopt this conference report . . . we will have at least taken a step in the right direction to solve the problem of aboriginal people in one of our states, and ultimately we will find that cost is very much less than it has been per capita for the natives in the lower 48. More than that, we give these people their birthright of individuality of freedom and dignity" (*Congressional Quarterly*, 1971, p. 2659).

The natives were concerned that, after 1991, individual shareholders would be able to sell their stock in the regional corporations. In February 1988, however, an amendment to ANCSA was passed making it impossible to sell or transfer stock unless the corporation itself votes to end this restriction. Whatever quarrel post-ANCSA critics have had with the legislation, it was a significant event in Indian policy history.

Its enactment both contributed to and expresses the shift in perspective favoring Indian interests.

Similarly, in 1972, the Passamaquoddy, Penobscot, and Maliceet tribes brought suit against the state of Maine for two-thirds of the state on the basis of the Trade and NonIntercourse Act of 1790. Subsequent court decisions in their favor—pointing out that the state had acquired Indian lands in violation of the 1790 statute requiring federal approval—forced the state to agree to a federal settlement in order to avoid protracted legislation and economic losses due to their inability to make land deals or generate state revenue as long as title to the land remained clouded (McLaughlin, 1977; Taylor, 1983).

The $81.5 million settlement, finalized in 1980, gave the tribes their right to 305,000 acres of woodland and a $27 million trust fund (*Congressional Quarterly*, 1980). The Maine settlement also illustrated that, however reluctantly, elected officials would uphold the view of the trust relationship that had established itself over the decade it had taken to settle the Maine Indian claims. In the words of Senator William Hathaway (R-Maine), head of the Maine congressional delegation at the time: "We can step in if a legislative remedy is available, but only at the request of both parties. If the government has a trust relationship with the tribes then the government has to look out for the Indians. That is the job of a trustee. The law is the law. If the Indians can prove their claim then they should get it. If they can't, they shouldn't" (McLaughlin, 1977, p. 84). The Indians, of course, did prove their claim.

The examples of allocation and reorganization, termination and self-determination policies, and claims settlements provided in this chapter, illustrate how the constitutional mandate on Indian affairs is an evolutionary principle that is constantly being redefined. Sometimes the mandate has been defined so that the problems created by Congress and the courts favor non-Indian interests. At other times, as during the 1970s, it has meant advocacy for Indian causes and a strict interpretation of the federal government's trust responsibility. Most importantly, the policy epoch that reached its height during the seventies established several policy-making principles still operative today.

Thus, the trust relationship, which is an essential component of the constitutional mandate on Indian affairs, provided justification for advocacy in behalf of Indian interests by the institutions of the federal government. Ambivalence over the Indian political status, another dimension of the mandate, was resolved by adopting self-determination philosophy in the legislation of Indian affairs. The constitutional question of how public versus private or majority and minority interests are to be fairly balanced and represented, a third dimension of the mandate, was dealt with by enabling those minority Indian interests best able to represent themselves to use the special access provided by the mandate on Indian affairs to successfully accomplish major legislative goals. In these respects, congressional attitudes that favored self-determination over termination, legislation over litigation, or advocacy for Indian policies, resulted in the institutionalization of policy-making principles that remain viable. Lest the reader has been lulled into supposing, however, that constitutional problems, or questions of justice and fairness in Indian affairs, have forever been resolved, a word of caution is in order.

Although Indian victories of the 1970s may serve as a model for how Indian constituencies may capitalize on systemic changes to promote their own interests in the future, they also indicate that the ability of Indian constituencies to take advantage of the constitutional mandate will be contingent on two conditions. First, the constitutional mandate does not automatically or even readily lend itself to the advantage of poor minority interests. In order to make policy-making processes work in one's behalf, a major lesson of the 1970s holds that one must have, or be able to garner, the material, leadership, and financial resources necessary to make one's voice heard in government. Tribes lacking in, or refusing to invest these resources in pursuit of their policy goals, or who may insist on solely relying on abstract appeals to the trust relationship or to honoring the treaties, may find that they will be unsuccessful in getting what they want.

Furthermore, the experience of the seventies also indicates that Indian constituencies who refuse, or are unable, to use electoral system mechanisms—interest group activity, for example—will be less likely to make gains in the policy arena. Indian policy-making apparently follows the same rules as other policy development. Thus, multiple factors—among them ideology, Congress, the executive, the judiciary, and interest group activity—must converge in such a way, and at an opportune time, such as prevailed during the civil rights era, for minority interests to impact the legislative process. The next chapter examines more closely how self-determination ideology came to be such a significant factor in bringing about a pro-Indian shift in Indian affairs in the 1970s. Importantly, the official adoption of self-determination ideology by the federal government illustrates the key role that can be played by presidents in Indian policy development.

NOTES

1. Felix's Cohen's *Handbook of Indian Law* is the most complete treatment of the relationship between law and policy available. The 1945 edition of the handbook, for example, lists 4,264 separate statutes having application to

American Indians (U.S. Commission on Civil Rights, 1973, p. 1); in addition, treaties were formally negotiated with the tribes, until 1871, adding to the legal base of Indian affairs; Chief Justice John Marshall's famous decision declaring the tribes' "domestic dependent nations," in *Cherokee Nation v. Georgia* (1830), is an example of a court decision whose meaning continues to be debated and interpreted in Indian policy circles. Article 1, Section 8, the "Commerce Clause," and Article II, Section 2, the "Treaty Clause," are sources of constitutional authority in Indian policy.

2. See Jackson and Galli (1977, pp. 95–97) for a mathematical example of what fractionated heirship looks like. Briefly, a land share is divided in such a way, through succeeding generations, that a contemporary Indian land holder might end up with a share as small as 1/235,450, or 3.7 square feet, in a twenty-acre allotment.

3. Deloria (1983, 1984), who is among the more prominent critics of the IRA, makes this point.

4. Indian resistance to termination policy is discussed in Svensson (1973, p. 31) and Josephy (1984, p. 132). An especially graphic account is given by Tyler (1973).

5. Pevar (1983, p. 32) estimated 650 treaties as the total number. Vogel (1972, pp. 162–163) estimated 372 treaties and 74 agreements (Brophy and Aberle, 1977, pp. 125–126). The Institute for the Development of Indian Law (1973) listed 415 treaties and 97 agreements. See also Cohen's (1982) *Handbook of Federal Indian Law*.

6. One of the more popular recent treatments of broken promises to the Indian, and the genocidal wars that were fought in the effort to confine Indians to reservations, can be found in Michener's (1974) *Centennial*.

7. Nixon fired Hickel on November 25, 1970, and appointed Rogers Morton in January 1971.

3

The Origins of Self-Determination Ideology and Constitutional Sovereignty

What policy specialists mean by "self-determination" is crucial for understanding Indian policy development in the 1970s. There were, however, several perspectives on self-determination that influenced their approach to Indian legislation (see Figure 3.1). Despite the variety of interpretations involved, policymakers nevertheless agreed that self-determination meant self-government for Indian tribes (66.7 percent) and economic development (69.7 percent) (see Table 3.1).

However, these tabulations do not show that the two definitions of self-determination are related, although on different sides of the same coin. Thus, for policymakers involved with Indian affairs during the 1970s, self-determination was the belief that Indian tribes and communities could become economically and politically autonomous by applying their powers of self-government to the pursuit of economic development and self-sufficiency. The policy community's consensus on this view of self-determination thus enabled quick and responsive action on Indian issues, especially after 1975. This was not the case before 1975 because the consensus was still being hammered out between President Nixon and Congress.

The view that self-determination meant economic development through self-government, however, was not everyone's. Thus, many

Figure 3.1
Perspectives on Self-Determination

	Political Sovereignty	Legal Sovereignty	Self-Determination	Self-Governance
Main Ideas	Independent/Nation Status	Honor Treaty Terms/Trust Relationship	Participation in Decision-Making Process/Contracting	Tribal Self-Government/Limited Jurisdiction
Proponents	Social Movement Organizations/AIPRC	Indian Legal Movement/Washington Representatives	President Nixon/Congress	NTCA/Indian Tribes
Strategy	Collective Actions/Militancy	Legal/Judicial Decisions	Legislative	Strengthen Tribal Government/Administrative Relationships

Table 3.1
Policy Specialists' Definitions of Self-Determination Ideology

Definition	Percent of Respondents Citing Definition[a] (N = 66)	Number of Times Mentioned in an Interview[b]	
		1 & 2	3 or More
Self-determination as economic development; self-sufficiency	69.7	44	28
Self-determination as self-government; powers of tribal self-government	66.7	44	53

[a]Percentages refer only to those respondents who cited the definition indicated. For example, forty-six respondents, or 69.7 percent of the total, cited economic development as a definition of self-determination; twenty respondents did not give economic development as a definition for self-determination.

[b]The number of times a definition was cited in the interviews is given here as a measure of the importance with which it was regarded by the respondents who mentioned it as a reason for the 1970s policy shift.

pro-Indian policy advocates held views that defined self-determination as legal or political sovereignty, or some combination of both. The legal sovereignty perspective emphasizes honoring the treaties, preserving the land base, and enforcing the trust relationship. Political sovereignty focuses on obtaining independence or separate nation status for the tribes.

All of these ideas about self-determination—as self-governance, or as legal or political sovereignty—had been around for some time, at least since the first treaties were signed. Thus, a central ideological innovation of the seventies was to contribute a new, minority, perspective that has come to define sovereignty in terms of the Constitution. This belief was first promulgated by the American Indian Policy

Review Committee (AIPRC). Its main tenet holds that the tribes are like the states and local governments in that they, too, have sovereign rights under the Constitution of the United States.[1] Although this view created significant controversy in 1977 when it was made public, and is still poorly understood, the notion of constitutional sovereignty has become increasingly influential both in legislating and in litigating Indian affairs.

The willingness of the AIPRC, and other minority advocates of the constitutional view, to go along with the prevailing definition of self-determination as economic development was probably related to strategic considerations. If so, it may have reflected a pragmatic awareness that policy would be easier to legislate if the more moderate, and not the more radical, perspective was espoused. The analysis of Representative Lloyd Meeds' rejection of the AIPRC's position presented in this chapter suggests this was indeed the case. Moreover, the constitutional perspective that emerged from the policy debate of the seventies can be traced to four origins: President Nixon's 1970 Message to the Congress, post–1975 congressional legislation, the American Indian Review Committee's *Final Report*, and to ongoing jurisdictional issues between the tribes and the states.

PRESIDENT NIXON AND CONGRESS DEFINE SELF-DETERMINATION

Policy specialists are generally in accord that the federal government's contemporary definition of self-determination dates from President Richard Nixon's Message to the Congress, on July 8, 1970. Coming as it did at the height of a climate of opinion favorable to the advancement of minority interests, self-determination ideology reflects a strong value for Indian participation in, and control over, the policies and programs that affect Indian life. Thus, the "romantic revolt" of the 1960s meant "identifying the powerlessness of the poor as the principal source of their inability to cope with their surroundings and break out of a 'culture of poverty' " (Beer, 1978, p. 26). The federal government's response was to try to empower minorities through the social programs of the War on Poverty and the philosophy of "maximum feasible participation."

It is within this context that policymakers defined a post–1975 perspective on self-determination. Thus, their emphasis was on creating opportunities for the Indians to participate in decision-making processes involving outcomes affecting their lives. Those few respondents who saw the president's message as an extension of the self-government philosophy of the 1934 IRA legislation are correct only in that the earlier legislation made it possible for Congress to begin to consider

Indians as entitled to the right of self-government. President Nixon's statement, however, went well beyond this recognition to suggest how the federal government might encourage real political autonomy for Indian communities, without severing the trust relationship.

In his opening remarks to Congress, and consistently throughout his message, the president made it clear that future federal policy should not continue to be paternalistic but "build upon the capacities and insights of the Indian people" (p. 101-A).[2] In order for this to occur, he argued, Congress must repudiate its terminationist and assimilationist biases. Moreover, the trust relationship should no longer be unilaterally defined but developed in consultation with the Indian people; "we must make it clear that Indians can become independent of federal control without being cut off from federal concern and federal support." Thus, termination policy, which had seriously undermined the trustee relationship, must be rejected because the premises upon which it rests are wrong. Here, Nixon argued that the trust relationship is a special relationship between Indians and the federal government and, as we have seen, one that is constitutionally and morally binding. The trust relationship will continue to mean that government owes the Indian in keeping with treaty and other formal obligations—but that from now on the relationship will be guided by egalitarian and sovereign, rather than paternalistic, principles.

Second, Nixon pointed out that the consequences of termination have been "clearly harmful"—that "their economic and social condition has often been worse after termination than it was before" (p. 101-A). Third, the president was aware that termination had created a great deal of "apprehension" among Indian groups and that, therefore, "any step that might result in greater social, economic, or political autonomy is regarded with suspicion by many Indians who fear it will only bring them closer to the day when the federal government will disavow its responsibility and cut them adrift" (p. 101-A). Accordingly, he stated, that:

Because termination is morally and legally unacceptable, because it produces bad practical results, and because the mere threat of termination tends to discourage greater self-sufficiency among Indian groups, I am asking the Congress to pass a new Concurrent Resolution which would expressly renounce, repudiate and repeal the termination policy as expressed in House Concurrent Resolution 108 of the 83rd Congress. . . . self-determination among the Indian people can and must be encouraged without the threat of eventual termination. In my view, in fact, that is the only way that self-determination can be effectively fostered. This then, must be the goal of any new national policy toward the Indian people: to strengthen the Indians' sense of autonomy without threatening his sense of community. (p. 102-A)

Even though President Reagan reaffirmed Nixon's position, in 1983, President Nixon's unprecedented disavowal of the termination policy significantly stands alone as the clearest, least compromised, rejection of this policy to date. Perhaps more than any other sentiment or proposal his statement contains, it served to persuade both Indian and Indian advocate alike that a new era had dawned for Indian policy.

In order to fully understand this point, we must remember that Indian preoccupation with the trust responsibility is central to any definition of Indian policy interests. The idea that government is constitutionally as well as morally obligated to protect the rights and well-being of the tribes is essential to the definition of the trust relationship as well as to the Indian claim of sovereignty. In the Indian conception, therefore, the trust relationship exists because treaties were once negotiated with them in recognition of their sovereign status as nations. Thus, to relinquish the trust relationship or to have it unilaterally abrogated by Congress, is equivalent to giving up or losing sovereignty.[3] This, as has become clearer since 1970, is precisely what Indians are willing to fight to prevent from happening.

As it turns out, in fact, Indian advocates—for example, Donna Harris, then wife of Democratic Senator Fred Harris (also an advocate in Congress) and an Indian leader in her own right, and, non-Indian advocates—like Senator Ted Kennedy, or academics like Edgar Cahn and Alvin Josephy, both of whom had written extensively on the subject of federal Indian policy abuse—were notably influential in developing the president's position on Indian self-determination, as were bureaucrats in the Department of Interior and the White House. During the 1970s, advocates were able to gain unprecedented access to Congress and the White House and so to bring their considerable political acumen to bear on questions of Indian policy and self-determination.

In the meantime, there is another sense in which the president's message to Congress was essential for the development of a consensus on self-determination. Nixon accompanied his statement with a list of concrete legislative and bureaucratic reforms that, if enacted, would further the goal of Indian self-determination. In fact, all but the Indian Trust Counsel Authority proposal were eventually passed by Congress. Those proposals on which action favorable to Indian interests was taken were: (a) that Blue Lake be restored to the Taos Pueblo; (b) that tribes be allowed to establish control over their educational programs; (c) that tribes be permitted to administer their own (Johnson O'Malley) educational funds; (d) that Congress enact financing legislation to guarantee loans to the Indians for economic development purposes; (e) that an Assistant Secretary for Indian Affairs be created in the Department of Interior; (f) to increase funds for Indian health; and (g) to support urban Indian centers. In justifying these proposals Nixon provided further clarification of what he meant by self-determination:

In the past, we have often assumed that because the government is obligated to provide certain services for Indians it therefore must administer those services. . . . there is no necessary reason for this assumption. Federal support programs for non-Indian communities—hospitals and schools are two ready examples—are ordinarily administered by local authorities. There is no reason why Indian communities should be deprived of the privilege of self-determination merely because they receive monetary support from the federal government. Nor should they lose federal money because they reject federal control. (p. 102-A)

Nixon's reasoning here is key to understanding not only the minority position on self-determination—that Indian communities should be treated like local governments—but also because it may explain Congress' delay in taking action on his proposals. In view of the president's strong rejection of termination policy and his support of greater powers of self-government for the tribes, his use of the hospitals and schools example is revealing and, as far as Congress might have been concerned, too extreme. The president, that is, appears to be saying that Indians are like other local authorities, by which he means state and local governments. Thus, Congress' resistance to enacting the president's proposals—it was five years before the Indian Self-Determination and Education Act was passed—was in keeping with the terminationist and assimilationist orientation that Indians would be better off free from the trust relationship that had evolved after World War II. To suddenly, after twenty years of believing that Indians were being assimilated, be asked to view Indian tribes as potentially sovereign entities, in the same way as states and local governments, was probably asking too much of Congress in 1970.

On the other hand, policy specialists appear to think that political factors, primarily in the nature of the rivalry that existed between a Democratic Congress and a Republican president, were partially responsible for the delay. They also argue that major legislative proposals are often years in the making before policymakers can be educated to the need for enacting them or before a combination of certain people and events are in place to make them happen. Although both of these reasons are cogent, especially in that major changes took place in Indian Committee chairmanships in the mid-seventies, it is difficult to explain Congress' delay in acting without referring to the ideological radicalness of Nixon's self-determination philosophy and therefore to the need to find a more moderate view before consensus could be achieved.

Given these constraints, when the Congress' endorsement of self-determination ideology finally did occur, in the Self-Determination and Education Act of 1975, it manifested itself in an operative, technical sense, not at all in keeping with the president's more radical sentiments. Congress' self-determination principle, known as *contracting*, is in keeping, however, with the notion that self-determination means economic development through self-governance. In contracting, tribes are able to decide for themselves when and how they will administer federal programs on Indian reservations. This principle enables dealing directly with federal agencies for the delivery of services to Indian communities. Implementation data on how contracting has worked are not yet available but they will probably show that most tribes are ill-equipped to take advantage of this option. Policy specialists are aware that most Indian communities lack the human, financial, and physical plant resources necessary to manage their own programs. Some Indians also feel that to act too quickly with respect to contracting may be to court termination.

Apprehension that economic and political self-sufficiency may lead to termination is always present in Indian country and is enjoying something of a comeback, given the backlash that has occurred in response to Indian treaty victories and because of federal budgetary cutbacks. With respect to Indian child welfare policies and programs, however, Indian tribes and communities have been exercising sovereign rights.

SELF-DETERMINATION AND INDIAN CHILD WELFARE

Of all the legislation enacted by Congress during the 1970s, the Indian Child Welfare Act (ICWA) of 1978 provides perhaps the purest and most comprehensive example of self-determination ideology at work.[4] The purpose of the legislation was to create new standards for the placement and adoption of Indian children in order to prevent the unwarranted removal of Indian children from their tribal environments and thereby to protect Indian cultural and tribal identity and integrity. Significantly, the act is a radical departure from historical practices in that it gives the Indian tribes, and not state governments, exclusive jurisdiction in child custody proceedings. It is this approach to questions of Indian child welfare that is in line with the view that the tribes have sovereign rights.

The ICWA requires the tribes to decide placement and adoption policies. Thus, preference must first go to a member of the child's extended family, then, to other members of the child's tribe, and finally, to another Indian family. Other provisions enable the states and tribes to work out their own arrangements on these matters and specify that grants should be made available to the tribes for implementing child welfare programs—for licensing operating facilities, staff training, and day-care schools, for example.

An examination of the Senate hearings that were held on this legislation in 1974 and 1977, as well as respondent opinions on the subject of the act, indicates that there was very little real opposition to the legislation. Having already become sensitized to Indian demands for self-determination, Congress was largely receptive to the request for greater tribal jurisdiction in matters of child welfare policy. We should note, however, that this policy is of the social welfare type and therefore less likely to be controversial than policies that legislate land and natural resources type issues, and involve non-Indian interests. If in this sense we therefore control for the type of policy, we find that the case for the ICWA was made largely on its merits. It is one of those rare instances where social science data and the statistics on the number of Indian children placed outside of tribal settings or Indian homes persuade policymakers and potential opponents alike that something must be done to protect Indian interests.

Toward this end, studies conducted by the Association on American Indian Affairs, the American Academy of Child Psychiatry, the American Indian Policy Review Commission, the National Tribal Chairmen's Association (a Department of Health, Education and Welfare contract for the study), and the North American Indian Women's Association (a Bureau of Indian Affairs [BIA] contract for the study) were singularly influential in making the case for Indian control. The statistics they contain—showing disproportionate rates for the placement of Indian children in non-Indian settings—are extensively cited in the hearings.

In addition to providing proof that discrimination and prejudice have been the rule in placement and adoption practices, the hearings reflect widespread emotional commitment to the ideal that Indian children are a tribal resource—its primary means of insuring continued survival and cultural integrity. Senator Abourezk, who chaired the hearings, for example, pointed out that there was "no reason or justification for believing that... Indian parents are unfit to raise their children, nor ... to believe that the Indian community itself cannot, within its own confines, deal with the problems of child neglect when they arise" (Hearings, Senate Subcommittee, 1977, p. 1).

The combination of statistical fact and emotional appeal resulted in a blanket indictment of government and private agency placement and adoption programs and personnel. It is an indictment with which few at the hearings were prepared to disagree, even the legislation's strongest opposition, the Church of Jesus Christ of Latter-day Saints (LDS or Mormon).[5]

No one, however, was more instrumental in making the case for Indian self-determination in child welfare policy than William Byler and Bertram Hirsch of the Association of American Indian Affairs. The association is a pro-Indian advocacy organization that has been in existence since the 1920s, and in this case, had been documenting abuses in Indian child welfare matters since 1967. Byler's report, an "Indian Child Welfare Statistical Survey" (July 1976), and Hirsch's subsequent work on the legislation itself, constitute remarkable examples of the influence that this "friend of the Indian" organization, and its two representatives, had on the development of legislation that was so obviously in keeping with Indian policy preferences. We return to the subject of non-Indian organizational and entrepreneurial influence in a later chapter.

This discussion of the ICWA illustrates how self-determination ideology influenced Indian policy development after 1975. It also suggests that, in addition to reflecting an operative consensus, the self-determination legislation contained the seeds of an alternative view, that Indian tribes are entitled to sovereign rights, like those held by the states. This position is best exemplified in the American Indian Policy Review Commission's *Final Report* to Congress in 1977.

THE AMERICAN INDIAN POLICY REVIEW COMMISSION TACKLES THE STATUS QUESTION

Although the commission endorsed the consensus on self-determination defined as economic development and self-government for the Indian tribes, its major contribution was to present the view that self-determination should mean considering the tribes a third unit of government within the federal system of states and the national government. Although not as radical a notion as the historical idea that tribes are separate nations, the view that tribes should be thought of as having the same sovereignty as states and local governments was met with a great deal of opposition. Despite this initial resistance to it, however, the idea that the tribes should be defined as constitutional sovereigns has caught on. President Reagan's Indian policy, for example, stipulates a "government-to-government" relationship with the tribes.

Still, the idea that tribes are constitutionally sovereign remains embryonic. It has yet to be defined legally, or to achieve consensus. Nevertheless, it may have already come to reflect the sentiments of an increasingly larger number of Indian advocates and communities. Because Indian policy development is importantly preoccupied with the question of political status, the origins of the idea of constitutional sovereignty are examined more closely.

An act creating the AIPRC was passed in 1975. The commission was to consist of three Senators, three Representatives, and five Indians. It was chaired by Senator James Abourezk (D-South Dakota) and the vice chairman was Representative Lloyd Meeds (D-Washington). In addition, Ernest Stevens, of the Oneida tribe, served as executive director of the commission and Kirke Kickingbird, of the Kiowa Tribe, as general counsel. The only other upper echelon staff member was Max Richtman, a non-Indian. By statute also, the eleven task forces, of three members each, were required to have a majority of Indian staff. Actually, however, thirty-one of the thirty-three task force members were Indian. Moreover, all of the commission's members at the time were widely regarded as Indian advocates.

The commission's purpose was to conduct a comprehensive study of the conduct of Indian affairs and it was to expire six months after the submission of its final report to Congress, or no later than June 30, 1977. Pursuant to its mandate, the commission conducted extensive hearings, in Washington and regionally, on a variety of subjects relevant to Indian affairs: the trust relationship, tribal government, federal administration, jurisdiction, education, health, alcohol and drug abuse, reservation development, urban Indians, Indian law, and political status. It published eleven task force reports and several special studies, for example, on Alaska natives and the BIA. Although it published 206 recommendations dealing with these topics, the commission's work is largely remembered for its controversial views on the nature of Indian status and for Congressman Meeds' public rejection of them.

Proponents of the AIPRC's conclusions agree with its view that "Indian tribes are governments . . . the federal policy must accept the position that the supervisory authority it asserts must be limited and flexible" (AIPRC, *Final Report*, 1977, pp. 100–101, pp. 103–107). Accordingly, federal policy should be aimed at

aiding the tribes in achievement of fully functioning governments exercising primary governmental authority within the boundaries of the respective reservations. This authority would include the power to adjudicate civil and criminal matters, to regulate land use, to regulate natural resources such as fish and game and water rights, to issue business licenses, to impose taxes, and to do any and all of those things which local governments within the United States are presently doing. (AIPRC, *Final Report*, 1977, p. 143)

In addition to these views, the commission concluded that the growth and development of tribal government into fully functioning governments necessarily meant exercising some tribal jurisdiction over non-Indian people and property, especially those within reservation boundaries (AIPRC, *Final Report*, 1977). In defense of its position, the commission pointed out that:

Tribal governments are emerging from an essentially dormant period forcibly imposed upon them by federal policies directed toward their ultimate destruction. The tribes are beginning to assert those governmental powers necessary to take their proper place in the role of governments within the United States. The powers they are seeking to assert are no more and no less than those of any local sovereign of these United States. The objectives they seek to attain are peace and tranquility within the reservation boundaries and economic independence which will permit them to operate free of the federal purse strings without fear of termination. (AIPRC, *Final Report*, 1977, p. 153)

The commission is clearly defining the tribes as equal to the states and other forms of local government. The response of other Indian groups, although not of non-Indian organizations, was generally favorable to this new definition of Indian status. Thus, in an otherwise qualified letter of support from the conservative National Tribal Chairman's Association, there is explicit endorsement of the commission's definition of Indian status. This letter stated that:

the Indian people will never surrender their desire to control their relationships both among themselves and with non-Indian governments, organizations, and persons.... Indian tribes possess the moral right to endure and shall do so as self-determining people.... It must not be forgotten that before the age of European discovery Indian tribes enjoyed complete mastery of the continent, governing their land and people as fully sovereign, self-determining policies. ... Thus, the Constitution expressly recognizes Indian tribes and identifies them as political entities separate from the states and foreign nations—to be dealt with as tribes (Article I, Section 8, Clause 3). (Chino and Townsend, 1977, pp. 570–572)

For the association, as for the commission, "The long-term objective of Federal-Indian policy 'should' be the development of tribal governments into fully operational governments exercising the same powers and shouldering the same responsibilities as other local governments" (AIPRC, *Final Report*, 1977, pp. 13, 143).

Meeds' lengthy dissent forcefully rejected these views and thus exemplifies resistance to the idea that Indian tribes may be seen as constitutionally sovereign. Meeds first accused the commission of "one-sided advocacy"; of seeking to "convert a romantic political notion into a legal doctrine" (AIPRC, *Final Report*, 1977, pp. 571, 391). In fact, as another memorandum to the commission pointed out, the commission was never intended to be objective:

Congressman Meeds...should know better than anyone else that there was not the slightest pretense of staffing the Task Forces with neutral people. Everyone was an Indian leader or well-known advocate of Indian causes. They were, in truth, expected to be Indian and tribal advocates...what was expected was the gathering of facts and arguments to express and document the tribal and Indian views. (Dellwo, 1977, p. 301)

Meeds went on to reject the proposition that tribes are like the states:

American Indian tribes are not a third set of governments in the American federal system. They are not sovereigns.... To the extent American Indian tribes are permitted to exist as political units at all, it is by virtue of the laws of the United States and not by any inherent right to government, either of themselves or of others. (AIPRC, *Final Report*, 1977, p. 573)

In one sentence, for which there is item-by-item rebuttal from a number of sources (AIPRC, *Final Report*, 1977), Meeds summed up the opposition's position on the AIPRC's version of Indian status. "The doctrine of inherent tribal sovereignty adopted by the majority report," he argued, "ignores the historical reality that American Indian tribes lost their sovereignty through discovery, conquest, cession, treaties, statutes, and history" (AIPRC, *Final Report*, 1977, p. 574).

Meeds also went to the heart of the matter by indicating that there is more at stake, in his view, than legal or philosophical arguments. He obviously believed that the commission's view of sovereignty, should it ever prevail, will do irreparable harm to non-Indians: "Doing justice to the Indians does not require doing injustices to non-Indians" (AIPRC, *Final Report*, 1977, p. 612, see also p. 579), and, "if Congress should ever think it wise to give Indian people experience in government by letting them practice on non-Indians, I predict we would be swiftly set straight by the vast majority of our constituents" (AIPRC, *Final Report*, 1977, p. 391).

Apparently, Meeds was strongly advised by his colleagues in Congress not to make public his disagreement with the commission's views. Nevertheless, by doing so, he affirmed the opinion of many policy specialists that Indian policy decisions will remain inconclusive so long as the question of Indian status remains unsettled. In Meeds' views, moreover, settling the question of sovereignty can be accomplished by Congress. The commission's position, on the other hand, implies that Congress should not legislate in regard to these matters—that sovereignty and the trust relationship are evolving doctrines best left to the courts and to "intergovernmental agreements" between the tribes and the states (AIPRC, *Final Report*, 1977, pp. 5, 143, 624).

As this discussion indicates, the commission's position, and Meeds' response to it, were rooted in very different interpretations of Indian sovereignty. The federal government, represented by Meeds' views, believed it has absolute authority in Indian matters and that, therefore, the tribes cannot have rights in the same sense that the Constitution reserves sovereign rights to the states. The commission, however, believed that the constitution already contained or, logically, by extension, might be amended to grant states' rights to Indian tribes.

Actually, the commission's interest in redefining the Indian's political status was entirely consistent, in view of the ambiguity with which Indian status has historically been defined. Thus, the idea that Indian tribes are "domestic dependent nations," from which government derives its authority over Indian affairs, has not been definitively interpreted, despite Supreme Court decisions that have, over time, extended the government's authority. It is this very absence of clarity with respect to the status of Indian tribes that makes the commission's position credible. In other words, as long as the federal-state-tribal relationship remains open to interpretation, then it will be possible to generate serious discussion, as the commission has, about the future nature of political relationships. In the words of one policy specialist:

Sovereignty was not an issue in the sixties but it was in the seventies. The Commission brought it front and center.... Sovereignty is the last thing the Congress wants to hear about for the next 200 years, but it's there.... In the meantime, the tribes are getting ready with brilliant lawyers, graduates from the best law schools...and they start winning cases on sovereignty in the courts. They are pushing it right up to the point where some Supreme Court Justice is going to have to say, "This is what Marshall meant...." When it's all over, who knows what will happen? There's frustration at the Court for not going all the way. But, how much, short of writing a new Constitution, can you go? Because that's what sovereignty would mean: "We the people of the United States and the Indian Nations."

One important source of ambiguity with respect to defining political status has been jurisdiction. In particular, the Indian political agenda continues to pose a serious challenge to state authority over tribal affairs.

STATE AND TRIBAL RELATIONS: HOW ARE THE TRIBES LIKE THE STATES?

State and tribal relations are typically questions over criminal and civil jurisdiction and the extent to which the tribes may be said to have power over the governance of their own affairs vis-à-vis states' rights. Current issues over which tribes and the states are in conflict include: criminal jurisdiction, water rights, land use and development, and gaming policies. Other issues involve the power to tax, license, and zone as well as to regulate hunting and fishing and other treaty rights (Hall, 1979; Medcalf, 1978; Pevar, 1983).[6] These are rights associated with sovereign status, so Indian rights may be expected to conflict with those of the state governments, who usually claim the same jurisdictional powers the tribes want.

Generally, the tribes have exclusive jurisdiction unless a treaty or a federal statute stipulates otherwise, and not because their rights are stated in the Constitution (Institute for the Development of Indian Law, 1983). However, despite instances where the states have been able to extend their power to tax or extend criminal and civil jurisdiction over the tribes, as through allotment policies, via PL 280, or in energy resource development, the states have been singularly unsuccessful in promoting their own interests over those of the tribes. For example, every state attempt to regulate activities involving only reservation Indians has failed either the preemption or infringement test that is required before a state can exert jurisdiction without congressional authority (Pevar, 1983).

The constitutional mandate on Indian affairs has thus meant that the federal government's trust responsibility extends to protecting Indian communities from intrusion by the states even when—as in the case of bifurcated briefs, land claims, water rights, or mismanagement by the BIA—the government has had to make the case against itself in order to protect Indian rights (Hall, 1979). In the 1970s, for example, two practices—*bifurcated* and *split* briefs—were instituted to enable Indian legal issues to be handled either directly by the Supreme Court, without going through the Department of Justice, as in the first example, or which required solicitors from the Department of Interior to present one set of arguments in behalf of the Indian position and another in behalf of the government's, as in the case of split briefs.

Despite these constraints, PL 280, enacted in 1953, seriously undermined tribal authority by allowing the states to extend jurisdiction to the tribes. PL 280 was limited by the Indian Civil Rights Act of 1968, but it has been viewed by many as "perhaps the most widely denounced federal Indian legislation in recent years" (Kickingbird, et al., 1983, p. 12). Similarly, the 1978 Supreme Court decision in *Oliphant v. Suquamish* has been widely viewed as a major setback for Indian criminal jurisdictional authority.

The Oliphant decision denied tribal courts' jurisdiction in cases where a non-Indian has committed a crime in Indian Country. Critics of the decision are afraid that the decision thus creates a new doctrine— that of "inherent limitations" on sovereignty—which may lead to even more negative consequences for the tribes, namely, by limiting the vision of constitutional sovereignty (Institute for the Development of Indian Law, 1983).

Even with these setbacks, however, the Institute for the Development of Indian Law has concluded that U.S. law "endorses Indian sovereignty and tribal self-government and generally supports the exercise of tribal jurisdiction in Indian territory" (Institute for the Development of Indian Law, 1983, pp. 7–8, 13–14). Such success, however, has not been accomplished without rigorous vigilance by Indian constituencies and often at great personal and financial cost. Indian hunting and fishing rights in Washington, and currently in Minnesota, for example, have been gained despite sometimes life-threatening opposition from non-Indians (Josephy, 1984). Moreover, as far as many are concerned, Indian successes on an issue-by-issue basis still do not resolve the all-important question of political status.

Similarly, in the example of Indian water rights, the extension of the trust principle to Indian-state relations has had the effect of helping the tribes resist encroachment of their water rights by the states. Particularly in the western United States, and in view of water needs related to technological and energy resource development, water is a precious commodity over which Indian and non-Indian interests are in direct conflict.

Although Indian water rights are protected by the treaties and upheld in the "Winters Doctrine" (*Winters v. U.S.*, 1908), the states have consistently tried to assert their own "prior appropriation" doctrine over Indian rights. Recently, these efforts have led to a push to quantify water rights that, if successful, would be detrimental to the interests of the tribes because quantification would require the tribes to use their water under conditions over which they would have less control.

Thus, although water rights cases may be heard in state as well as federal courts, pursuant to the 1952 McCarren Amendment, Indians have chosen to litigate in federal court, with some success. The northern Paiute victory with respect to Nevada's Pyramid Lake, Truckee River, dispute is an example (Josephy, 1984). Furthermore, Indian success in federal court has helped to sustain their opposition to national quantification policies that would mandate a legislative solution over questions about who gets how much water. So far, Indian opposition has held up enactment of such legislation, first proposed in 1981. Moreover, since 1982, Indian groups have attempted to bring together a coalition to protect Indian water interests.

Gaming policies, bingo games and other types of gambling on Indian reservations, are another area in which the tribes have successfully opposed the infringement of state jurisdiction over tribal affairs and kept alive the question of their sovereignty. Ever since reservations introduced bingo as a way to accomplish economic development, states have opposed the right of the tribes to regulate gambling operations. Nevertheless, Indian persistence on this issue has led to favorable court decisions as in *California et al. v. Cabazon Band of Mission Indians et al.* (February 1988). Currently, several bills that would designate which activities may be regulated by the tribes and which by the state, and to establish a National Indian Gaming Commission are before Congress.

These examples illustrate how issues of political status have been exemplified in state-tribal relationships. As illustrated elsewhere in this study, Indian activism, buttressed by the federal mandate to protect and enhance Indian interests, has helped to keep sovereignty questions at the forefront of the Indian affairs agenda. It remains to be seen if a consensus on constitutional sovereignty will establish itself, thus extending the view of self-determination that has prevailed in the Indian policy arena since the early 1970s.

In the meantime, and although policy specialists are very much aware of the nuances in meaning that accompany the debate on sovereignty, there is no agreement about how the question of constitutional sovereignty will be resolved. The Reagan administration's Indian policy, however, does spell out the contradictions that need to be resolved:

When European colonial powers began to explore and colonize this land, they entered into treaties with sovereign Indian nations. Our new nation continued to make treaties and to deal with Indian tribes on a government-to-government basis. Throughout our history, despite periods of conflict and shifting national policies in Indian affairs, the government-to-government relationship between the United States and the Indian tribes has endured. The Constitution, treaties, laws, and court decisions have consistently recognized a unique political relationship between Indian tribes and the United States which this Administration pledges to uphold...by removing obstacles to self-government and by creating a more favorable environment for development of healthy reservation economies. (Friends Committee on National Legislation, 1984, p. 4; Press Release, 1983)

Close examination of this text reveals an inconsistency between the rhetoric claiming a government-to-government relationship and the emphasis on economic development and self-government that, we have seen, expresses the old view of self-determination and not the emerging consensus on constitutional sovereignty for Indian tribes. Furthermore, President Reagan's inability at the Moscow summit on arms control to remember his own words on tribal sovereignty suggests that, so far, the government's new policy has been rhetorical.[7]

The main thrust of the Reagan administration's Indian policy, the work of the Commission on Reservation Economies, has been to affirm the view of self-determination as economic development and self-government, not as a third form of government. Future debates on Indian sovereignty will continue to grapple with these definitional issues.

NOTES

1. For instance, the AIPRC's *Final Report* lists forty recommendations in support of greater powers of self-government for Indian tribes and forty-four in support of economic development policies. Together, these recommendations account for 43 percent of the total; obviously, both self-government and economic development policies are basic components of the self-determination philosophy, but not the definition the AIPRC chose to emphasize.

2. These quotations, and those that follow, are from President Nixon's Message to the Congress, *Congressional Quarterly Almanac* (1970), pp. 101A–105A.

3. That the Indian policy community equates sovereignty with self-government and the trust relationship can be seen in the AIPRC's *Final Report*, pp. 100–103, 622.

4. This discussion of the legislation is taken from the hearings before the Senate Subcommittee on Indian Affairs, 1974 and 1977; House Report 95–1386 (July 24, 1978); and Senate Report 95–597 (November 1, 1977).

5. The Mormon church (LDS) was prominently represented in the hearings, because its adoption programs were frequently cited as a primary example of the historical trend to remove Indian children from tribal to non-Indian home environments. Citations to the AIPRC in this chapter are from the *Final Report*, 1977.

6. Jurisdictional power is, for example, the power to license, tax, or zone as well as the assertion of treaty rights in regard to hunting, fishing, leasing, and economic development in general.

7. President Reagan's remarks to Soviet students drew criticism from American Indian leaders. Reagan, for example, said the American people made a mistake when they gave Indians reservations rather than integrating them into society. He went on to betray his ignorance that American Indians have been U.S. citizens since 1924 by commenting that "we should not have humored them in ... wanting to stay in that kind of primitive lifestyle ... we should have said: – 'No, come join us. Be citizens along with the rest of us.' " The president also mistakenly referred to Indians as "very wealthy because some of those reservations were overlaying great pools of oil. And you can get very rich pumping oil" (*New York Times*, 1988, p. 7, A13).

4

Federal Spending and Indian Self-Determination

Policy specialists identified a number of ways in which federal spending during the Great Society/War on Poverty era influenced Indian policy development (see Table 4.1). Thus, Indians acquired influence through community action and education programs, through the creation of "Indian desks," and generally, by taking advantage of the new programs created by federal funds to create decision-making structures that were alternatives to dominance by the Bureau of Indian Affairs (BIA).

Several of the sources of influence mentioned by policy specialists, namely, "poverty spending," "developing Indian leadership," and "spending as an alternative to BIA dominance" emphasize the view of policy specialists that federal spending was more important for its less tangible and long-term effects than for its immediate benefits. Thus, although concrete program benefits were important, federal spending also facilitated the development of Indian leadership and the establishment of a new Indian political base on the reservations and in the cities. In other words, federal spending for Indian programs in the 1960s and 1970s helped create the Indians' new "political clout" and thus established self-determination as the basis for Indian policy development. This chapter examines this thesis by explaining how these

Table 4.1
The Influence of Federal Spending on Indian Policy Development

Source	Percent of Respondents[a] (N = 66)	Number of Mentions[b] (Times Mentioned)	
		1 and 2	3 or More
Poverty program spending	53	31	41
Spending for education	34.8	25	17
Indian leadership development	34.8	26	7
Throwing money at the problem	33.3	27	10
Indian desks	27.3	28	6
Spending as an alternative to BIA dominance	21.2	13	3

[a]The numbers and percentages reported here refer only to those respondents who cited the source. For example, thirty-five respondents remarked on poverty program spending, which means that thirty-one of them did not.

[b]The number of mentions is a measure of the importance respondents attached to the variable in question. Multiple mentions indicate emphasis and suggest importance.

developments were associated with spending during the War on Poverty era.

THE NEW FRONTIER, GREAT SOCIETY, AND WAR ON POVERTY PROGRAMS

President Kennedy began the era of spending for social programs with New Frontier proposals aimed at eradicating poverty.[1] American minority populations were quickly shown to be the poorest of all, and so, early on, the government's focus was on enacting special legislation for minority communities. Kennedy's response to poverty in Indian Country was to appoint a task force, in 1961, headed by Philleo Nash, to establish the Area Redevelopment Administration (ARA). The ARA made the tribes eligible to sponsor their own programs, and thus was a precursor to the contracting legislation enacted in 1975.

Nash also viewed the ARA as an opportunity to funnel more funds to the reservations. Thus, tribes were able to build community centers and tribal buildings, both of which helped establish a physical base for political activities. Moreover, the ARA's philosophy was to enable the Indians to help themselves, that is, to become empowered through participation in program decision-making processes and by managing these programs themselves. This new community organization concept was made a major feature of the War on Poverty programs enacted after 1964.

Nash also urged abandoning the termination policy. In 1961, for example, he persuaded the BIA to permit Indians greater control over its programs. Thus, Indians became involved with economic development strategies aimed at bringing new industries to the reservations, with housing authorities, and education programs. But the most immediate effect of the new approach was to make an unprecedented amount of money available to the tribes.

By 1967, the number of new industrial enterprises on or near reservations had doubled, from 21 in 1963 to 110 in 1967.[2] Moreover, they provided more than 9,000 jobs, with an additional 1,344 Indians involved in on-the-job training programs. By 1968, another 8,000 Indians were involved in government-sponsored adult vocational training, up from 2,911 in 1963. The controversial relocation programs were spending $40 million by 1972 in order to help Indians find homes and jobs in 8 large cities.[3] Similar increases in spending occurred for public works employment and the development of Indian business enterprises.

Despite these efforts, the Kennedy administration did not succeed in putting termination to rest. The tribes were well aware that Kennedy had failed to protect Seneca interests in the matter of the Kinzua Dam, which was built despite sustained Indian protest. As one respondent observed, the Kennedy administration had "promised more than it could deliver." Nevertheless, money flowed onto the reservations and developed a momentum for change of its own.

Federal Spending for Education

More money for Indian education meant additional grants and scholarships, thus enabling many more Indians to enroll in programs for higher education. In 1969, for example, financial assistance from the BIA totaled $3 million, enabling 3,500 Indians to go to college. But, by 1974, government was subsidizing education for 13,500 students at a cost of $47 million in loans, grants, and other funds, $26 million of which was directly in the form of BIA scholarships (Levitan and Johnson, 1975). Moreover, the fact that by 1974 nearly every tribal government also made scholarships available had added another $3 million to the pot (Jackson and Galli, 1977). In addition, combined state, local, and federal expenditures for Indian elementary and secondary education were more than double the average per student nationwide (Levitan and Johnson, 1975).

Significantly, those Indians who would later assume leadership roles in the War on Poverty and on the reservations, graduated from these programs. They were to play a key role in bringing about the pro-Indian shift in policy development. In explaining the influence of Alaska natives, one respondent expressed it in the following manner:

The third thing you have to have is a Native elite—well educated in the White sense and capable of acting on behalf of older people and the general mass . . . as their legitimate representatives. They came out of military service and college and, although from Chilocco and Chemawa [Indian schools], more than anything else, they came from Mt. Edgecombe High School in Sitka because there were no high schools in the villages until the State was forced to begin building them in 1966. Through the fifties it was a massive high school, totally limited to Natives, and a boarding school which took children at a critical age and at great psychological expense. But they went at the behest of their families and of officials who really pushed education. And they got their education, although I'm not sure it's what the BIA had in mind. And out of that came a generation of young people, now in their forties, who formed the land claims political elite. They're all there in the yearbooks, all the leaders—in their gym suits and high school pictures—now bankers and stockholders: senators and representatives.

Poverty Programs and the Development of Indian Leadership: The Lawyers

Lyndon Johnson continued federal spending for Indian economic development and education through the War on Poverty programs created by the Economic Opportunity Act of 1964. These programs were aimed at poverty populations and were also a way to carry out the equal opportunity provisions of the Civil Rights Act, which was enacted in the same year. Thus, the Community Action Program, Legal Aid, Headstart, and Job Corps were created, along with special desks in the departments of government, intended to meet the needs of Indians.

The goals of Indians who held an American Indian Capitol Conference on Poverty in 1964 were, therefore, to ensure that the new programs would reflect Indian values and cultural preferences (Josephy, 1971). In this respect, War on Poverty programs were a new breakthrough for the idea that Indians should become politically empowered by participating in the design of programs that would be congruent with their own cultural needs and policy interests. Indian desks, for example, were department of government "set-asides" that earmarked funds for Indian projects. Consequently, they were a regular budgetary item and, thus, an important and reliable source of funds for everything from housing to road and dam construction projects. Therefore, when Indians successfully carried out these and other poverty programs, they contributed to the belief that there were alternatives to doing it the BIA's way. As one policy specialist put it, "Everything follows logically from the decision to give money directly to the tribes and from the fact that Indians running their own programs was not a disaster."

Indian poverty programs were a conspicuous success. Legal aid programs, for example, were controlled by the tribes and thus were an important vehicle for representing Indian policy preferences. The Navajo legal aid program, Dinebeiin a Nahiilona be Agaditahe (DNA) or "Attorneys That Contribute to the Economic Revitalization of the People" was a culturally sensitive program in that attorneys had to satisfy tribal requirements in order to practice, including continuous residence on the reservation for at least four months before applying for a tribal license. In addition, the twenty-two person policy board of directors was made up of a majority of tribal members (Deloria, 1983). Despite having also to be approved by the Department of Interior and the Commissioner of Indian Affairs, these legal aid programs were instrumental in defining and defending Indian preferences.

Other Indian organizations originated from poverty program spending. The Native American Rights Association (NARF), for example, began as a California Legal Aid Program in 1970. Currently, NARF handles approximately 200 cases a year, and has a legal staff of 17 attorneys, two-thirds of whom are Indians. Recently, NARF has played a major role in bringing land claims suits to the courts for the eastern tribes, Maine among them. In 1979, although 28 percent of their funding came from private sources, 59 percent still came from the federal government (Deloria, 1983). NARF also operates an Indian Law Support Center, which provides for consultations with tribal attorneys, and an Indian law library.

In fact, the new breed of attorneys that emerged from the War on Poverty era—idealistic and energetic in their pursuit of justice for Indian causes—has been enormously influential in helping to represent Indian policy interests (Deloria and Lytle, 1983; Svensson, 1973).[4] Both Tom Tureen, the lawyer who represented the Maine Passamaquoddy and Penobscot tribes, and Reid Chambers, who served in the Solicitor's office and now privately represents Indian clients, are non-Indian advocates who became involved with Indian affairs through the poverty programs.

Policy specialists also observed that the number of Indian lawyers increased significantly. Although actual numbers are difficult to pinpoint, because not all Indian lawyers practice Indian law, the increase has been substantial. The University of New Mexico Indian Law Program, for example, estimated 500 in 1984. Other estimates put the number of Indians who are lawyers at 100 in 1975, and at almost 1,000 in 1985 (Richard Truedell of the American Indian Lawyer Training Program, Oakland, California, quoted in Lichtenstein, *The New York Times*, 1975, p. 31, and Friends Committee on National Legislation, Summer 1984, respectively).

Furthermore, the era's lawyers are found today in the Department of Justice, the Attorney General's office, and the Department of Interior, to name only a few federal government employers. Significantly, many more have gone into private practice and represent Indian clients. One respondent summed up their impact this way:

In some ways the last fifteen years have been the period of the lawyers. We have done what we can do legally. We have built a base in Congress. The law is well-established—there are no longer unanswered fundamental questions. It's like the period of the social workers was in the 30s, and that of the soldiers in the late 1800s. The point is they [Indians] are using some professional groups within the dominant society to do things for Indians—that hasn't changed.

Community Organization and Indian Leadership: The Indian Community Action Program Directors and Staffs

The establishment of Indian Community Action Programs (ICAPS) on the reservations figured prominently in generating new employment opportunities for educated Indians who otherwise would have had to stay away. Moreover, the poverty program community development philosophy emphasized helping people to help themselves. Thus, policy specialists viewed the ICAPS as having provided Indian leadership a place from which to operate and to try and do for the tribes what it had previously been left for the BIA to do.

Before the ICAPS was established in 1965, the primary sources of employment for Indians were the BIA, the Indian Health Service (IHS), and the tribal bureaucracy. Thus, employment opportunities were severely limited and required conformance to civil service standards. Because most tribes also lacked viable economic enterprises—a lumber mill, coal mine, or factory—which might offer employment opportunities, Indians who were benefitting from the new educational programs had to leave the reservations to make their careers.

The ICAPS, with their generous budgets and competitive salaries, were able to attract this population. It also helped that most Indian programs, then as now, had preferential hiring policies. Thus, an Indian leader like LaDonna Harris, for example, was able to organize the American Indian Opportunity Organization, which began as an Oklahoma poverty agency. Peter MacDonald, who had been educated as an engineer, returned to the Navajo Reservation to head its ICAP. He became Tribal Chairman and was especially influential during the Nixon and Ford administrations.

Other Indian leaders who rose to prominence during this time were John Stevens and Charlie Edwardsen. Stevens, a Korean War veteran and Passamaquoddy Indian, was instrumental in instigating the Maine land claims suit. Like others during the War on Poverty era, he used civil disobedience tactics to fight discrimination on the reservation. In 1966, for example, he led a sit-in opposing construction on a site contested as belonging to the Indians (Directions, "People of the Dawn"; McLaughlin, 1977).

Edwardsen also rose to prominence through Office of Economic Opportunity programs in Alaska. Poverty program money, for example, helped create the native regional associations, which in turn endorsed political candidates and were a factor in the Alaska land claims movement (Berry, 1975; *Civil Rights Digest*, 1969). Even Ross Swimmer, Principle Chief of the Cherokee Indian Nation, co-chairman of President Reagan's Commission on Reservation Economies, and recently Commissioner of Indian Affairs, became reinvolved on the reservation through his interest in housing projects and poverty programs in the late sixties and early seventies (Daviss, 1984).

These examples point out that much of the tribal leadership viewed as so effective in advancing Indian policy interests during the seventies got its start through poverty programs. Thus, as one respondent observed, "Had there been no War on Poverty there would have been no opportunity for educated and experienced Indian people to come home and find an outlet for their abilities. As a result, educated Indians began focusing on the scope and extent of their sovereignty and on a reexamination of their treaty rights."

In their endeavors, Indian leaders were buttressed by the legitimacy of a community organization philosophy that believed that they should decide their own destinies. Consequently, they took advantage of increased opportunities to influence policy decision-making processes. Their success in promoting Indian causes thus served to convince their Indian constituencies that governmental policies detrimental to their interests could be changed. Federal spending, as one respondent put it, was "a horse which Indians rode all through the seventies," and with the very important effect of permanently changing the course of Indian affairs. As one policy specialist observed, "You won't reverse the court victories or de-educate the Indian lawyers—the feeling that things can change."

FEDERAL SPENDING: AN ALTERNATIVE TO BIA DOMINANCE

Most of the effects of federal spending for Indian community development were straightforward. Large amounts of money went for services and to generate employment opportunities. More importantly, however, the legitimacy of the self-help philosophy meant that Indian communities could experiment with self-governance with renewed vigor and commitment. That the new Indian leadership did just this brought about the era's greatest benefit: an enhanced confidence in the Indian's own ability to determine policy outcomes and the conviction that, from now on, Indians would play a major role in Indian affairs. In the composite view of several respondents:

The poverty programs revised thinking in this country . . . these weren't Indian programs but Indians got in on them—it was the first time they were ever given their own money, as opposed to the BIA giving them whatever they get, and them limping along on too little . . . they made for community awareness, a sense of self-importance and strength—the attitude that we're not going to take it any more. . . . Now, a tribal chairman could be paid full-time, he didn't have to drive a truck forty hours a week and go home at night to work off the kitchen table. This enabled the formation of tribal units that could function as effective . . . governments.

Although benefits of this nature are hard to quantify, policy specialists had no difficulty in naming this new attitude as a significant departure from the past. Thus, the importance of the belief that there was an alternative to the dominance of tribal affairs by the BIA must be understood in historical context.

Congress' trustee authority over Indian tribes has traditionally been administered by agencies of the federal government. The BIA, which has been delegated primary responsibility for carrying out Indian policy, was officially created in 1834. The BIA's role in tribal affairs has always been controversial. Criticism of the BIA has varied considerably, focusing sometimes on self-aggrandizing Indian agents and at other times on bureaucratic mismanagement and inefficiency. Historically, however, there has been some consensus that the BIA's disposition to view Indians as childlike wards of the government led to the implementation of policies that were paternalistic and caused dependence on government programs. Thus, the BIA has been viewed as undermining the trust responsibility and Indian policy interests. In Edgar Cahn's words:

From birth to death his home, his land, his reservation, his schools, his jobs, the stores where he shops, the tribal council that governs him, the opportunities available to him, the way in which he spends his money, disposes of his property, and even the way in which he provides for his heirs after death—are all determined by the Bureau of Indian Affairs acting as the agent of the United States Government. (Cahn, 1970, pp. 4–5)

By 1970, criticism of the BIA had become pandemic; as a result, in part, of the rejection of paternalism by minority populations in the civil rights movement. Thus, the psychological consequences of dominance by the BIA meant that many Indians had become totally dependent upon the BIA for their social, economic, and political well-being and, even worse, resigned to the inevitability of their exploitation. Indians had come to believe there was little, if anything, they could do to resist the status quo.

The challenge to these deeply rooted attitudes of resignation and despair came, as we have seen, on several fronts. Thus, federal spending created programs and opportunities that the War on Poverty philosophy required Indians to operate. Poverty program money also enabled Indians to get together at conferences and exchange views and strategies for social change, without having to have permission from the BIA. A new pan-Indianism emerged as one alternative to BIA dominance.[5]

One caveat to the thesis that federal spending fostered a viable alternative to the BIA's control of Indian affairs, is the argument offered by Piven and Cloward that government largess actually buys off or coopts leadership. Thus, movements that appear to pose a radical threat to the existing social and political order are said to become compromised when they accept money for new programs or their leadership accepts highly salaried positions.[6]

I conclude that the Piven-Cloward hypothesis does not fit the experience of American Indians in the 1970s. The goals of Indian activists, even those of the militants, were to honor the treaties that had been made with previous generations, not to create an American revolution. Thus, Indian social movement goals were often reactionary and traditionalist in that they called for a return to the old ways of Indian life, before contact with the whites. At the same time, the political philosophies of some of the radical leadership—to replace capitalism with socialism, for example, or to establish separate Indian nation states within the United States—were by no means widely shared in Indian Country, most of which remained staunchly patriotic. The American Indian Movement's confrontive, sometimes militant, take-over and shoot-out strategies nevertheless furthered a common perception that Indians held revolutionary ideals.

Although Indian traditional ways might indeed have a radicalizing effect if they were to be imposed on American society, there was no Indian political party or ideology systematically espousing this end at the time. Instead, Indian movement goals demanded ending BIA control by restoring sovereignty to the tribes. Sovereign practices, of course, were to be defined as the tribes chose.

On the other hand, the Piven-Cloward hypothesis does help explain why so much money was funneled into minority communities at times of greatest social upheaval. James Button, for example, has shown that federal agencies greatly increased the flow of monies to communities that like Watts, Buffalo, or Detroit, experienced significant racial violence (Button, 1978, chaps. 1–3). Although Indian communities were also the beneficiaries of federal spending, they were much more likely to exercise their considerable political acumen in hearings, as community organizers, and as lobbyists than on the streets.

In the cities, for example, Indians established urban Indian centers using federal funds. These provided a base for making needed services available to urban Indian populations and served to draw public attention to their problems. Thus, Indians were able to become a visible ethnic minority, to a degree not possible before the War on Poverty era. Most collective Indian actions of the late sixties and early seventies had this urban environment as their political base.

From the political bases of the cities and reservations, however, Indians developed social change goals that were well within constitutional and electoral systems' norms. By doing so, they effectively enhanced their capacity to achieve Indian policy change objectives. In taking advantage of Office of Economic Opportunity and Great Society funding and affirmative action programs, for example, Indians were able to get educations, to find employment, and to create their own alternatives to the BIA's power over, and management of, Indian affairs. Thus, in convergence with other factors examined in this study, federal spending contributed to the foundation of a new "can-do" attitude in Indian Country and therefore to the pro-Indian shift in Indian policy development.

NOTES

1. The Kennedy administration was influenced in this respect by the publication of Michael Harrington's *The Other America*, which precipitated a major public dialogue on the extent of poverty in America.

2. The statistics in this section are taken from Jackson and Galli (1977, pp. 120–130), unless otherwise cited.

3. The relocation program was ended in 1972 but aid to urban Indians continued under the name of Employment Assistance.

4. According to Frances Svensson (1973), passage of PL 280 "alerted many of the young people active in national Indian politics to the critical need for Indians trained in law." (p. 34).

5. I am using "pan-Indianism" here to describe establishing a new political identity for Indians that attempts to transcend particularistic tribal and cultural needs in behalf of common goals (Thomas, 1977, p. 739).

6. See Piven and Cloward (1971) in which they develop the theory that government expenditures for social programs will increase with an increase in widespread social unrest. For a case analysis using this thesis, see their discussion of the black civil rights movement in Piven (1977, pp. 181–263).

5

Presidential Initiative and Indian Policy Development

HOW PRESIDENTS INFLUENCE POLICY PROCESSES

Policy specialists are very much aware of the impact presidential policies have on Indian affairs legislation. Seventy-one percent of them emphasized the importance of policy statements and fifty-three percent commented on the value of administrative actions taken in support of those policies (see Table 5.1). Prior to the modern era, however, few presidents had shown much personal interest in Indian affairs. Franklin Roosevelt's Indian policy, for example, was largely the work of Commissioner John Collier, although Roosevelt's actions in support of Collier's initiatives were helpful in obtaining enactment of the 1934 legislation (Tyler, 1973; Tyler, n.d.).

Presidents Washington and Jefferson, on the other hand, were centrally involved with rationalizing and promoting Indian legislation, particularly the benchmark Indian Intercourse Acts of the 1790s. As Prucha and others pointed out, their intentions were to protect the Indians and the settlers from each other.[1] Thus, although they did not succeed in preventing war with the Indians, their policies laid the groundwork for current eastern Indian land claims actions.

In the 1830s, President Andrew Jackson also figured prominently in the Indian affairs of his day but his policies are widely regarded as

Table 5.1
Sources of Presidential Influence

	Percent of Respondents Who Mentioned Source[a] ($\underline{N}$ = 66)	Number of Times Mentioned in an Interview[b]	
		1 & 2	3 or More
Presidential initiatives: Messages, executive orders, speeches, task forces, campaign priorities, formal policy	71.2	43	79
Presidential support: Political appointees to executive agencies, reorganization of the BIA, leadership of administration officials and White House staff	53.0	32	31
Access to the White House under Richard Nixon: Special assistants, White House staff, special meetings, receptivity to Indian experts, advocates	36.4	27	26

[a]Percentage of respondents indicates only those who cited the source.

[b]Number of mentions refers to the number of times the source was mentioned by those citing it and suggests emphasis or intensity.

having been detrimental to Indian interests. Thus, in 1831 and 1832, Jackson defied Supreme Court decisions that sought to protect Indian territorial boundaries from the states and enacted a removal policy. This removal policy forced eastern Indian nations from their homelands via a "Trail of Tears," which was so named in acknowledgment of the deaths, starvation, and deprivation that accompanied the forced removal of the Cherokee, Choctaw, Creek, Seminole, and others to the Oklahoma Territory (Forman, 1932).[2]

As Jackson's example illustrates, American presidents in the nineteenth century were far more concerned with opening the continent to settlement, and with the nation's mandate for manifest destiny, than with the protection of Indian rights. Furthermore, in the twentieth century, the Roosevelt administration's strong support of Indian interests was offset by President Eisenhower's tacit endorsement of the termination policy designed by Senator Arthur Watkins. President Nixon's Indian policy thus constituted a major breakthrough for Indian interests. In many respects, his stands alone as having had the greatest influence in molding today's self-determination approach to Indian affairs by advancing Indian policy interests.

Policy specialists indicate that presidents may advance Indian policy interests in three ways. First, presidents are influential when they present highly articulated, and visible, policy statements. Thus, presidents may focus attention on Indian affairs by making special messages to the Congress, as did Johnson and Nixon, or they may issue executive orders and create special task forces and commissions to study Indian matters and propose changes, as did Kennedy, Johnson, and Reagan. In taking these actions, presidents announce to Congress and the American public that they are making Indian policy a major priority and indicate the direction they wish it to take. In this way, presidents may set the tone for their administration's position on an issue and thus persuade others that they intend to follow through. As one respondent said of Kennedy's Indian policy: "There was an executive coloring book on everybody's desk at the time which had a cartoon which said, 'color me important.' And color the Indians important is what we intended to do—it was very deliberately and carefully done." President Nixon, moreover, was personally committed to his Indian policy and took political risks in support of it.

Second, presidents may influence Indian affairs through administrative actions in support of their policy. Thus, through their appointment powers, they may place advocates or detractors in a position to advance or stymie the development of a pro-Indian agenda. Nixon, for example, appointed Walter Hickel to be Secretary of Interior with the understanding that Hickel would appoint Indians and Indian advocates to leadership positions in the Bureau of Indian Affairs (BIA), which he did. And President Kennedy noticeably advanced Indian interests with the appointment of Philleo Nash to be Commissioner of Indian Affairs and Stewart Udall as Secretary of the Interior. Nash, of course, was instrumental in laying groundwork for Indian participation in the conduct of tribal affairs. Udall was responsible for the land freeze that catalyzed action on the Alaska land claims. President Reagan, continuing the preferential hiring policies implemented by Nixon, appointed Ross Swimmer, Principal Chief of the Cherokee Nation, to be Assistant Secretary of Indian Affairs.

Third, presidents are influential when they go beyond "standard operating procedures" and provide special interests with unprecedented access to the White House. Thus, in the Nixon administration, congressional liaisons and special assistants for Indian Affairs were expected, sometimes to their own discomfort, to push for legislative solutions responsive to Indian policy preferences.

Access may also be provided Indian interests through special councils and commissions whose purpose is to provide a forum for Indian views and develop proposals for change. Presidential administrations since Kennedy, except for Carter, have each established such councils and commissions. Johnson's creation of a National Council on Indian Opportunity was a major contribution in this regard because the council was later revitalized, under Vice President Agnew, to serve Indian policy views. Recently, President Reagan established a National Commission on Reservation Economies for the purpose of developing strategies for achieving economic self-sufficiency on the reservations.

It fell upon Richard Nixon, however, to pull these various sources of influence into an integrated perspective on the development of Indian policy. In doing so, he succeeded in convincing Congress and the bureaucracy to adopt self-determination ideology in the formulation and implementation of Indian policy. In promoting this new Indian policy he therefore advanced the Indian policy agenda and forced the government to be responsive to Indian needs and respectful of the trust relationship. Nixon's was thus a major accomplishment of the 1970s policy era in Indian affairs and deserves closer examination.

NIXON TAKES OVER: THE PRESIDENT'S INDIAN POLICY

Nixon's commitment to the trust mandate—to the principle that Indians were sovereign participants in the legislation and operation of Indian affairs—was the final event in a chain of presidential initiatives that had begun with the War on Poverty. Nixon's approach to Indian affairs thus had the fundamental impact of changing the way both Congress and the bureaucracy viewed their roles. The result, in Congress, was to replace the bias for termination with a value for self-determination, in keeping with the idea that Indians had a right to decide their own destinies. The effect of Nixon's policy on the bureaucracy was to ensure, through preferential hiring and appointments to upper echelon administrative positions, that Indians would represent themselves rather than be represented by the BIA, as in the past.

Nixon's administration accomplished these results in several ways. First, in his campaign promises and message to Congress, Nixon laid out an Indian policy agenda that the administration then strongly pursued. As a result of such persistent advocacy, by 1975, Congress had enacted most of these proposals, leading to greater Indian control over tribal programs.

In addition, the Nixon administration revitalized the National Council on Indian Opportunity, thus enhancing White House access to Indian views. The NCIO played a prominent role in helping to negotiate an end to the Indian occupation of Alcatraz Island. It also developed proposals for extending federal services to urban Indians. The council's major contribution to the development of a pro-Indian agenda, however, may have occurred with the appearance of Vice President Agnew, Chairman of the Council, Secretary Hickel, and Commissioner of Indian Affairs, Louis Bruce, at the October 29, 1969 Annual Convention of the National Congress of American Indians.

At this time, Indians were already aware that, in a 1968 campaign appearance in Omaha, Nebraska, the president had indicated Indian affairs would be a matter of highest priority for his administration. Thus, in 1969, they were interested to find out how the president planned to proceed. Agnew accordingly stated the administration's intentions to resolve the Alaska claims, develop Indian leadership, respond to the needs of urban Indians, attack the economic problems of reservations, and preserve the trust relationship. The NCIO, for example, Agnew stated, is "the first time in the history of federal-Indian relations that the Indian people have had this type of official recognition and representation" (Strickland and Gregory, 1970, p. 434). Hickel, an unpopular appointee, nevertheless also contributed the statement that theirs would not be a pro-termination administration. Bruce, in his turn, emphasized the need for an intergovernmental relations unit and for restructuring the BIA.

These statements, known as the "Albuquerque Declarations," were significant because they accurately portrayed the course of action that was followed by the Nixon administration. In July 1970, for example, Hickel transferred the responsibility for reservation BIA programs to the Zuni tribe, thus beginning a practice that was finally made official in the self-determination legislation of 1975. Agnew's commitment to greater access through the NCIO was given expression through the participation of Indian advocates like William Veeder, Alvin Josephy, and others, in formulating Indian policy. Josephy, for instance, produced a document that became the basis for Nixon's BIA reorganization policy. LaDonna Harris, and White House and BIA officials, worked with the NCIO to produce the president's 1970 Message to the Congress.

The commitment to developing Indian leadership was carried out, in part, by creating the National Tribal Chairmen's Association (NTCA) in 1971. The NTCA was viewed with suspicion by many who saw it as an instrument of the BIA and a spokespiece for the administration. Nevertheless, the NTCA provided tribal chairmen with increased access to the White House and enabled some of them to take bolder positions on policy issues than they otherwise might have.

The administration's commitment to reorganize the BIA was carried out under Hickel. Its primary thrust was to appoint Indians to high status positions in the BIA. Louis Bruce, who became Commissioner of Indian Affairs, for example, was a Mohawk-Sioux from New York and a Republican. Bruce brought with him a new crop of activists—popularly known as the Katzenjammer Kids—who are credited with having shaken up the BIA, contributing to the pro-Indian shift by giving the administration of Indian affairs a pro-Indian slant. Other "movers and shakers" frequently named by policy specialists included Leon Cook, Director of Economic Services; William Veeder, water rights; Browning Pipestem, Ernie Stevens, Alex McNabb; Morris Thompson, Special Assistant for Indian Affairs; and Harrison Loesch, Assistant Secretary for Public Land Management.

Respondents suggested that the attempt to reorganize the BIA was constrained, but not stopped, when Hickel was replaced by Rogers Morton, by Loesch's opposition to Indian interests after the 1972 takeover of the BIA, and because of the opposition from the old guard in the bureaucracy, especially with respect to shifting the BIA's role from a management to a services orientation. Notably, the BIA's reorganization was a strong statement in support of preferential hiring practices and resulted in an innovative and energetic agenda favoring greater Indian participation in and control over policy development and implementation processes, changes that are still underway today.

With respect to land claims and treaty rights, the administration came through on promises to restore Mt. Adams to the Yakima, Blue Lake to the Taos, and on Menominee restoration. The political dynamics associated with the restoration of Blue Lake provide an especially illuminating example of how the Nixon administration dealt with the opposition and acted as an advocate for the Indian cause.

The Taos Pueblo of New Mexico had been engaged in a sixty-year battle, since 1906, to reclaim 48,000 acres of land that had been placed in the Carson National Forest. The lands taken included Blue Lake, a site that had religious significance for the Pueblo. The Nixon administration was aware of the issue's potential significance for negating the president's anti-Indian image. Thus, the assignment to "do something" about Blue Lake had been given, at John Erlichman's instigation, to Bobbie Kilberg. She, in consultation with LaDonna Harris, the NCIO and others, had worked out a strategy for returning Blue Lake to the Taos. Several respondents stressed the symbolic significance of this issue for explaining the administration's credibility and effectiveness in Indian policy; consequently the story may best be told in a composite narrative of their words:

What people didn't know about Blue Lake is that it was the time of the ABM vote and Clinton Anderson [Senior Senator from New Mexico] couldn't stand the Taos Pueblo.[3] It wasn't just concern about the precedent it would set—he was very emotional and threatened to vote against any agreement to return Blue Lake and maybe take Gordon Allott [Interior Committee Senator from Colorado] with him. In fact, at one point we had it [the Self-Determination Message] printed up and ready for release. We'd obtained all the numerous sign-offs when [a White House Aide] came running into the press room yelling, "Pull it, Clinton Anderson is gonna vote against the ABM for sure." So we did, and this delayed the message two weeks. But Richard Nixon overrode us saying, "This is important; it's the right thing to do," and, "go ahead, don't worry about Anderson." But we brought the Taos people in and we decided to have a big meeting with some of the Secretaries, and others, to take pictures. Well, the next day it turned out to be on the front page of the *New York Times*, July 8, 1970. Everyone had applauded and Erlichman was very pleased at the reaction. He saw it as good for the President...with this kind of favorable publicity we knew we HAD to do Blue Lake then. We beat back Jackson to do it.... We lobbied the Senate and wrote speeches and the Democrats worked out of Fred Harris' office. What happened was that the Senate Committee goofed. They overlooked a leasing detail and this enabled us to beat the Committee on the floor of the House. Our own congressional liaison didn't want to have anything to do with it. It was the first time in the history of the Interior Committee that the Chairman had been overruled.

The floor fight in the Senate was incredible. We flew people in. Even gave Senator Mathias a state police escort so he could get there on time. He had an accident on the way, but made it. And we sat the Taos Pueblo people in the balcony and they sat there and stared straight ahead and said nothing. Then Goldwater took the floor. He had refused to talk with us and we had no idea what he was going to do—our hearts were in our throats. Then he said, "I've watched the Taos struggle and I think we should even turn Phoenix over to the Indians, so the least we can do is support this measure." The cacique then stood up and raised the cane Lincoln had given them. There was complete silence on the Floor and then applause.

For the signing ceremony, the White House didn't want Kennedy and Harris, the co-sponsors, there [because they were Democrats], but Erlichman overruled them. A prayer was said in Tewa. It was very dramatic. Richard Nixon sat there, mesmerized, almost in tears. At one point, someone tried to interrupt him with a message but he waved them away.... He made his own extemporaneous statement—about having to be somewhere else later to talk about justice, but about how this was really where justice was being done. The

President was terribly moved...we were all weeping. That success made us fly.

The Taos Pueblo reclaimed Blue Lake in 1971.

As with Blue Lake, the Nixon administration had to overcome Bureau of the Budget opposition to the Alaska claims settlement. In the Senate, Henry Jackson, Chair of the Interior Committee, was already supportive of Native preferences on the issue. Moreover, so that the pipeline construction and land selections could proceed, there was pressure from oil interests and from the state of Alaska on the administration to settle the issue.

In the meantime, however, Secretary Morton, who replaced Hickel in 1971, had taken the position that the settlement should involve three million acres, instead of the forty million that had finally been agreed to by native interests. What happened next involved a highly charged meeting between Morton, the BOB (formerly Bureau of the Budget; now, Office of Management and Budget), Erlichman, and other principles. This meeting has been described as follows:

At the meeting Morton, who was a big, kind man, but who didn't know anything about Indians, said, "Three million acres is Interior's position." Erlichman looked him right in the eye and said, "The President wants forty million acres and X dollars." So, Morton immediately said, "Okay, then Interior's position is forty million acres and X dollars."

Afterward Erlichman was asked if the president had really told him that, in exactly those words. He is said to have replied, "the President said to do what's right...go on now, don't ask any more questions."

These examples illustrate, as others also could, the president's willingness to take risks in behalf of advancing Indian causes. Just as importantly, they illustrate how influential the Nixon White House staff was in developing and carrying out the intent and substance of the administration's Indian policy. The extensive liberties enjoyed by the White House staff in carrying out the president's policy provided them with a degree of influence meriting a more detailed discussion.

Richard Nixon was obviously committed to initiating and supporting the development of a pro-Indian shift in Indian affairs. Nevertheless, as one respondent put it:

It was Erlichman and Hickel who decided these things. Domestic policy bored Nixon. The foreign policy people could get an hour with him, anytime. The domestic policy people could hardly get five minutes. So you sent to Interior for the information but it got done in the White House by Erlichman. It was a closed system because that's the way the President was comfortable.

Consequently, it was White House staff who, either through personal interest, as in the case of White House Fellow Bobbie Kilberg, or by special assignment, as in the case of Leonard Garment or Brad Patterson, took initiative for seeing tribal delegations or preparing memoranda on the issues. That they were so successful is due largely to the thoroughness with which they permitted Indians and Indian advocates to play a part in their plans.

Indians and Indian experts became conspicuous visitors to the Nixon White House. As one respondent phrased it, in commenting on the staff's motivation:

Peter MacDonald and other tribal leaders were people we saw a lot of. Our relationships tended to begin with crisis situations but spilled over to other policy areas. There were all kinds of Indian leaders, from incrementalists to showboaters, but they were all important and made a contribution because they articulated what it was they wanted from us. And the fact they resented government condescension and paternalism struck a responsive chord with us.

In addition to providing access to Indian interests, White House staff also managed linkages with the executive departments. In this respect, they were willing to, and capable of, exerting pressure in behalf of their Indian policy goals. Kilberg, for example, once intervened with the Department of Labor to extend the Concentrated and Employment Training programs (CETA) to urban Indians.

Staff also worked to create a nonpartisan approach to Indian affairs in that Democrats were granted access to the Republican White House. LaDonna Harris, then wife of Democratic Senator Fred Harris, was an example of this strategy, as was the composition of the NCIO or the appointment of Reid Chambers to the Solicitor's Office in Interior. Chambers also had a reputation as an activist and had caused the government some concern before being appointed for his expertise in Indian law.

Partisanship, however, did prove to be a barrier in appointing a Commissioner of Indian Affairs. In this case, finding qualified Republican Indians was a problem and it was Senator Allott, not the administration, who acted to prevent naming any Democrats.

In an important sense, the question of how much of the Nixon policy was Nixon's, or that of his creative and zealous staff, is moot. The president's willingness to back his staff's initiatives, as demonstrated in several of these examples, made it possible for them to act as boldly, and with as much confidence, as they did. A more pertinent question, perhaps, is to ask why Nixon was so committed to fundamental change in the course of Indian affairs.

RICHARD NIXON'S COMMITMENT TO INDIAN POLICY

Respondent interviews tell a fascinating story of Nixon's involvement with Indian affairs. This is nowhere more evident than in their
speculations about a question many of them have asked: Why Nixon?
Although none of them claims a definitive answer, the reasons they
give for Richard Nixon's interest are worth noting. They tell us something about who the president was, of course, but they also reveal how
significant a role personal interest and commitment can play in determining the direction policy matters will take, especially when they
come from a president.

Most of the policy specialists who commented on this question think
that Nixon's desire to refurbish his anti-Indian, anti-minority, image
was behind his interest in American Indian causes. Nixon was widely
perceived as an enemy of civil rights legislation and had spoken against
racial integration as government policy. Other campaign references,
however, indicate that Nixon saw the Indians as disinclined to pursue
their civil rights through collective actions, of which he also disapproved. Indeed, respondents agreed that the Indians lost the president's
support when, despite the administration's best efforts, some Indians
occupied the BIA building and later engaged in the military action at
Wounded Knee.

Some respondents suggested that "Nixon always had a good feeling
for Indians. He always believed they had the short end of the stick,
and that they hadn't mastered the art of organization and protest like
other minority groups, so they could use the government's help." In
fact, Nixon's "good feeling" for the Indians was compatible with his
Republican values. He therefore could support policies indicating that
the Indians wanted to be separate and determine their own destinies
and not assimilate. Thus, Nixon's own values—for cultural and ethnic
segregation, for the right to a homeland, for decentralized decision-
making structures, and for Republican values, like justice and fairness—were congruent with those of the traditional Indian world view.
The Indian preference for tribal control, for example, was compatible
with Nixon's value for community control, which also played out in
the administration's revenue-sharing and decentralization policies.

These observations are persuasive and go a long way toward explaining the administration's choice of Indians as their minority group
to champion. However, nothing quite explains President Nixon's willingness to risk himself on the question of Indian causes as well as his
own words. In the following quote, Nixon describes the influence his
college football coach had on his development:

College football at Whittier gave me a chance to get to know the coach, Wallace
"Chief" Newman. *I think that I admired him more and learned more from him
than from any man I have ever known aside from my father.*

Newman was an American Indian, and tremendously proud of his heritage. Tall and ramrod straight, with sharp features and copper skin, from his youngest days he was nicknamed Chief. He inspired in us the idea that if we worked hard enough and played hard enough, we could beat anybody. He had no tolerance for the view that how you play the game counts more than whether you win or lose. He believed in always playing cleanly, but he also believed that there is a great difference between winning and losing. He used to say, "Show me a good loser, and I'll show you a loser." He also said, "When you lose, get mad—but get mad at yourself, not at your opponent."

There is no way I can adequately describe Chief Newman's influence on me. He drilled into me a competitive spirit and the determination to come back after you have been knocked down or after you lose. He also gave me an acute understanding that what really matters is not a man's background, his color, his race, or his religion, but only his character. (Nixon, 1978, pp. 19–20 [my italics])

In view of Nixon's own acknowledgment on the matter of Coach Newman's influence, it is quite possible that he may have vowed to do something for the Indians if he were ever in a position to do so. He was apparently quite distressed that a coach of Newman's stature had been denied access to the big leagues because he was an Indian.

Finally, Nixon's upbringing as a Quaker may have played some part in affirming his conviction that Indians were special. The Society of Friends has a long tradition of advocating in behalf of Indian rights and Nixon may have been introduced to this ethic as a child. In the end, whatever his motivation, it is clear from the evidence that Richard Nixon made a singular contribution to the development of the pro-Indian policy orientation that took root during the 1970s.

PRESIDENT REAGAN'S INDIAN POLICY

President Reagan's Indian policy extends self-determination ideology in the tradition of President Nixon and the American Indian Policy Review Commission. It also continues to reflect the historical ambivalence with which the federal government has regarded the question of Indian political status. Thus, in the press release of January 4, 1983, which preceded the president's official policy statement of January 24, 1983, the president's rhetoric affirms the "self-determination through economic development and self-government" philosophy laid down in the Kennedy and Johnson years. At the same time, however, Reagan makes explicit the sovereignty principles that importantly influenced the views of Nixon and the American Indian Policy Review Committee (AIPRC): "Just as the federal government deals with states and local governments in meeting the needs of other citizens, so should the federal government deal with tribal governments in promoting the well-being of American Indians . . . by removing obstacles to self-government and by creating a more favorable environment for development of healthy reservation economies" (Press Release, 1983). Thus, in addressing the political status of Indian tribes, the president expresses the federal government's new willingness to transact with the tribes as governments, thereby fostering the view of constitutional sovereignty that emerged from the AIPRC's work in the 1970s.

Two of the Reagan administration's mechanisms for achieving the government-to-government objective have involved naming a tribal representative to the Advisory Commission on Intergovernmental Relations, and designating a White House Office of Intergovernmental Affairs as liaison for the tribes. The latter action was accompanied by the observation that in moving this function from the White House Office of Public Liaison, "The President recognizes that tribal organizations are governments rather than interest groups such as veterans, businessmen, and religious leaders" (Press Release, 1983).

Such explicit attention to the question of political status for Indian communities—that they are governments, not just interest or minority groups—tremendously advances the views of many Indians and Indian advocates that the tribes are sovereign entities. Significantly, the progress that has occurred on the question of political status since 1970 (see Chapter 3) has fundamentally redefined the nature of the federal-Indian trust relationship in contemporary Indian politics. Arguably, therefore, the findings of this study argue for the conclusion that national policy-making processes have subsequently come to represent the interests of Indian constituencies in a way that is more consistent with democratic principles than has historically been the case.

Nevertheless, President Reagan's Indian policy also shows that the question of political status has not been definitively resolved. This point is clear from the government's continued focus on economic development as the means for achieving self-sufficiency rather than political independence. Thus, the Reagan policy talks about Indian tribes as governments but does not then logically proceed to discuss strategies for extending tribal jurisdiction or for legally and politically redefining the status of tribes. What presidential initiative and support since 1970 has therefore accomplished is to bring the question of political status to the foreground and thus to achieve some degree of acceptance for the idea that tribes are more than just wards of the government or one more minority group to attend to. It remains to be seen how much more closely the Indian and non-Indian conceptions of sovereignty will come to resemble each other in practice.

In the meantime, the idea that self-determination is sovereignty of some kind has become institutionalized in the way the federal government approaches Indian policy development. Thus, the continued cultivation of certain political behaviors by Indians—among them interest group activity, bipartisanism, and the capacity to use electoral system processes—has become essential to their ability to represent themselves at the national level.

NOTES

1. Bernard Sheehan, for example, argued that the Jeffersonian conception of the Indians was the prevailing philosophy toward Indian Affairs, even through Jackson's presidency. By this, he means that Washington policy makers believed that, whereas the Indians could not survive in their natural state, they would survive if civilized. The enlightened white men of the time thus held an essentially humanitarian, and optimistic, view of the Indians' future. Although they did not believe that the Indians could retain their cultures, in any case, they did believe that civilization and assimilation were preferable as well as inevitable. As Prucha also observed, their views were not compatible with those of the settlers and developers and, to this day, many Indians continue to resist adopting "The White man's ways" (Sheehan, 1973).

2. For a later defense of Jackson's Indian policy see Prucha (1969, pp. 527–539).

3. Hickel observed that Anderson was opposed to the vote because he was protecting the timber and down-river water users' interests in his state (Hickel, 1971, p. 174).

6

Congressional Advocacy in Indian Affairs

INSTITUTIONAL FACTORS

The Congress of the United States is a major actor in Indian policy development because it has a constitutional mandate on Indian affairs. Fully 86.4 percent of the policy specialists interviewed for this study agreed that members of Congress were responsible for the pro-Indian policy shift that occurred in the 1970s. This chapter examines in what ways respondents attributed influence to Congress; in particular, how congressional leadership and institutional factors aided the achievement of Indian policy goals and objectives.

Table 6.1 lists the seven variables most frequently cited by respondents in describing the sources of influence on Indian policy development in the seventies. Of the variables listed, three describe the important role played by legislators and their staffs in advocating for Indian interests ("members of Congress," "congressional staff," and "committee leadership"), two indicate the importance of representing one's policy preferences well ("merits of the case," "the legislation itself"), and one—"congressional committee pursuing its mandate"—affirms the significance of ideology in Indian affairs. A seventh variable, the "congressional backlash," serves to illustrate, by way of negative

Table 6.1
Sources of Congressional Influence on Indian Policy Development

Source	Percent of Respondents[a] ($\underline{N}$ = 66)	Number of Mentions[b] (Times Mentioned)	
		1 and 2	3 or More
Members of Congress	86.4	42	124
Merits of the case	69.7	50	40
Congressional staff	54.5	45	29
Legislation itself	54.5	44	25
Congressional Indian Committee pursuing its mandate	53.0	42	21
Congressional backlash	53.0	37	17
Committee leadership	47.0	32	25

[a]The percentage indicated refers only to those respondents who explicitly mentioned the source--for example, fifty-seven respondents (86.4 percent) mentioned members of Congress. Therefore, nine (13.6 percent) did not explicitly mention this source and are not shown in the table.

[b]Number of mentions refers only to those respondents who mentioned the source. Number of times mentioned refers to how many times during an interview the source was cited times the total number of mentions and suggests intensity and importance. For example, in the perception of those fifty-seven respondents who mentioned this source a total of 166 times, members of Congress are very important indeed to Indian policy development.

example, the importance of playing by the rules of the game. In these respects, policy specialists are arguing that a dynamic that might be labeled "congressional politics" should be considered in developing policy strategies. Furthermore, this chapter shows that the values elected officials have for getting re-elected, for not irrevocably alienating one constituency (non-Indians) in favor of another (Indians), or for making good public policy, will make a difference in their willingness to support legislation (Benham, 1977; Fenno, 1973).

Most of the variables cited by respondents as sources of congressional influence in Indian affairs refer to the characteristics of the Congress as an institution. In their turn, institutional norms and characteristics are regarded as important for understanding congressional decision-making processes. Thus, whereas we might expect members of Congress to be influential because they are supposed to make public policy, legislators will nevertheless tend to be most favorably disposed toward those proposals that are well researched, sponsored by the appropriate committee, and that do not unnecessarily alienate important constituencies. With respect to its adherence to institutional norms, therefore, we can expect Indian and general public policy processes to be quite similar. However, this study suggests that Indian policy development possesses additional attributes unique to Indian affairs.

For example, respondents clearly believe that Indian policy development benefited from the value legislators have for fairness; in particular, from the guilt many feel regarding the unconscionable treatment Indians have received. In fact, guilt was given as an explanation as much for the willingness of Republicans to support federal spending for Indian programs as for the inclination of eastern liberals to support Indian causes.

Similarly, congressional Indian committees provide Indian advocates with opportunities unprecedented in the policy-making system. Thus, with respect to what J. Leiper Freeman termed the "bureau-committee subsystem" of relationships between the committees, the BIA, and Indian constituencies—in addition to the Indians' special access through the constitutional mandate—Indian constituencies have a unique opportunity to make their policy preferences known (Freeman, 1955). No comparable structural advantage exists for any other subpopulation in American society. In view of these systemic advantages, therefore, we might well ask why Indian interests have not fared better in Congress than they had before 1970.

Until recently, Congress viewed the BIA, rather than Indian tribes and organizations, as the legitimate representative of Indian interests. The justification for this has been that the BIA was created to carry out Congress' trusteeship in Indian affairs. Therefore, Congress has expected the BIA to know what was best for protecting and enhancing the interests of Indians. After 1968, and the onset of Indian activism and the civil rights era, however, Congress, like other critics of past practices, came to view the BIA with suspicion and mistrust.[1] This view was reinforced, in the 1970s, by evidence of BIA paternalism, mismanagement, and even malfeasance in the administration of Indian affairs. As one respondent put it, the BIA acting as trustee resulted in "maps which had been lost, surveys that were wrong, even rivers . . . had been lost."

Self-determination ideology thus expressly rejected the paternalistic practices and assumptions that had historically guided Indian affairs and helped bring about Congress' present value for having Indians represent themselves in the policy arena. Congress' new perspective on Indian affairs eventually came to pervade its entire approach to Indian affairs. Thus, committee relationships, individual advocacy, and the dynamics of lobbying all shifted in the direction of creating a more favorable environment for the Indian voice than had previously been the case.

INDIAN COMMITTEES AND INDIAN COMMITTEE LEADERSHIP

Committees are essential to policy-making processes. They are how the complex work of the Congress is managed. Research also shows that committee leadership generally determines what the policy agenda will be, as well as whether it is responsive to constituency influences. Thus, the support or advocacy of committee chairs on the issues is singularly important in policy development. The behavior of Indian committees and their chairs in the 1970s appears to have conformed to this rule.

Richard Fenno's conclusions that Interior committees (with which the Indian committees have historically been affiliated) value serving their constituencies and making good public policy also apply to Indian policy development (Fenno, 1973; Benham, 1977). Thus, although committee members are always interested in their reelection chances, this goal is tied to meeting constituency needs, which have historically been pro-Western and pro-suer. In fact, only 12.1 percent of respondents suggested that Indian committee members might be more interested in reelection than in providing good service to their constituencies. Moreover, when, as happened in the seventies, committee chairs become the advocates, as well as managers, of good public policy, the effects can be remarkable.

In the 1970s, the chairs of Indian and Interior committees, like Henry Jackson and James Abourezk in the Senate, and Wayne Aspinall and Lloyd Meeds in the House, contributed to the development of the pro-Indian shift in policy development by becoming advocates for policy solutions furthering Indian preferences on the issues. In addition to taking helpful actions on specific issues, these leaders were especially effective because they knew how to balance the competing, frequently contradictory, claims of Indian and non-Indian constituencies so that, most of the time, no one constituency became too alienated from the policy process. Their leadership was largely instrumental in staving off a backlash to the pro-Indian policy shift until after 1978.

The ability of the chair to balance competing interests was especially remarkable because, prior to the seventies, serving constituency interests nearly always meant meeting the needs of non-Indians: the ranchers, farmers, miners, land developers, water users, and local governments who had historically leased or regulated the use of Indian lands for their own purposes. In fact, before 1970, Indian constituencies were so insignificant in policy development that they were virtually invisible.

In his otherwise exemplary study of congressional committees, Fenno, for example, does not talk about the Indian subcommittees at all. He therefore mistakenly observes that no one of Interior's clientele groups is more powerful than any other (Fenno, 1973). In reality, Indian clientele interests had historically lost out to those of non-Indian constituencies. Nevertheless, Fenno is correct in pointing out that the job of the Interior committee had been to protect the interests of commercial land and water users, which typically did not include considering Indian preferences (Fenno, 1973). After 1970, however, this relationship became notably more responsive to Indian constituency views. Moreover, in addition to the adroitness with which they managed Indian and non-Indian conflicts Indian committee chairs took important actions in furtherance of Indian policy preferences. Why they chose to take the political risks associated with becoming advocates for Indian tribes and organizations is worth a closer look.

As chair of the Senate Interior Committee, Senator Henry Jackson was instrumental in bringing about the Alaska Native Claims Settlement Act in 1971. Nevertheless, he was generally viewed as anti-Indian until his political aspirations became, as one respondent phrased it, "presidential."[2] American political traditions, it seems, require presidential candidates to be sympathetic to "the Indian problem." Art Buchwald, for example, includes "make no mistake about this, I'm for the American Indian" on his list of standard campaign rhetoric.

Whatever his motivation might ultimately have been, Jackson was responsible for forcing Interior Secretary Hickel's support of the Alaska land freeze until a settlement with the natives was reached. In addition, Jackson appointed Forest Gerard, a Blackfoot Indian, to the Senate Committee's staff. Gerard, along with his counterpart in the House, Franklin Ducheneaux, a Cheyenne River Sioux, ably applied committee mechanisms and congressional norms to giving Indians a voice in policy development.

Wayne Aspinall, Chair of the House Interior Committee, also applied his considerable stature with his colleagues toward successfully resolving the Alaska claims and in Indian, non-Indian jurisdictional disputes. Neither Jackson nor Aspinall, however, came close to approaching the fervent advocacy and success of James Abourezk, who took over Senate Indian affairs in 1974.

Abourezk's advocacy of Indian causes may have stemmed from his childhood on the South Dakota Indian reservation where his parents were traders. He is also a member of the American Arab minority and this fact may have intensified his unusual sensitivity to Indian points of view. Whatever the cause, Abourezk was instrumental in bringing Indian policy preferences to the forefront of the Senate Indian Committee's agenda.

Respondents pointed out that Abourezk came to the Senate intending to be a one-term senator. If so, then this fact goes a long way toward explaining why he chose to act so boldly in behalf of Indian causes. Other respondents, however, argued that his openly pro-Indian bias, especially his endorsement of the controversial sovereignty principle contained in the American Indian Policy Review Committee's (AIPRC) *Final Report*, made him so politically vulnerable that his reelection was probably impossible anyway. One anonymous respondent skeptically dismissed Abourezk's idealism this way: "Abourezk's family problems suddenly became so great he couldn't run again. He knew he would have been licked, so his family problems got bigger than they'd been."

In support of Abourezk's idealism, it should be pointed out that he took enormous risks in advancing a pro-Indian agenda. He would not have done so had a career in the Senate been his primary goal. Abourezk's decision in this regard may have been helped by the fact that senators are elected for a six-year term. This gives a senator more time in which to have even a one-time impact than do the two-year terms of House members.

Leadership initiatives favoring Indian interests in the House of Representatives were moved along by Lloyd Meeds, a Democrat from Washington State, who replaced Wayne Aspinall as head of the Interior and Insular Affairs Committee, which was responsible for Indian affairs. Aspinall's legacy of strong leadership enabled Meeds, at least for awhile, to advance Indian interests more quickly than might otherwise have been the case. Meeds was especially vocal in defending Indian hunting and fishing rights and with respect to articulating the new self-determination philosophy. Meeds' break with the Indians, after 1976, deserves attention because for many years he was viewed as a partisan of Indian causes. In part, Meeds' disenchantment with Indian causes, after 1976, is illustrative of the argument that there are real limitations to constituency advocacy in Congress should one group come to be perceived as having obtained unfair advantage over another.

The first of the events that contributed to Meeds' withdrawal from

Indian advocacy had to do with settling a dispute between Indians and non-Indians over fishing rights in Washington State. Indians had claimed prior treaty rights to regulate their own fishing. Non-Indians insisted that Indians should be governed by the same state hunting and fishing laws that applied everywhere else. The issue was settled, in 1974, after ten years of litigation and bitter conflict, in favor of the Indian petition. By 1976, therefore, it had become clear that Meeds' support of the Indian position might cost him reelection. He won that year by only a few hundred votes. Then, in 1978, opposition to his pro-Indian image was so strong that Meeds decided not to run for reelection. That year, Meeds' district elected an anti-Indian representative, Jack Cunningham, to the House.

The second event that contributed to Meeds' demise was his opposition to the AIPRC's *Final Report*. In this case, Meeds attempted to temper his pro-Indian image by taking a strong position against the Indian view on self-determination. His strategy backfired. Thus, although he was advised against taking such a strong stand by his congressional colleagues, Meeds insisted on publicly rejecting the pro-sovereignty views of the commission. The end result of Meeds' action was to alienate Indian groups, adding them to those non-Indians who already disapproved of his views on fishing rights. Isolated politically, Meeds had no choice but to drop out of electoral politics.

Meeds' experience illustrates, as does that of Abourezk, that there are limits to congressional advocacy. If advocacy is perceived as unbalanced—in other words, as unfair vis-à-vis favoring the interests of one constituency over another—then opposition will mobilize in an attempt to restore equilibrium to the policy process. As becomes evident, the emergence of a backlash in congressional Indian affairs was also importantly connected to rejecting the view that Indians are politically sovereign. Meeds and Abourezk's definitions of self-determination were therefore perceived as unacceptably too close to the idea that tribes are sovereign governments.

Their own political fortunes aside, Abourezk and Meeds clearly helped to create a favorable environment for Indian policy interests in Congress. Obviously, after generations of benign neglect and/or outright hostility toward Indian preferences, this was a significant accomplishment. Furthermore, the congressional value for doing the right thing, respondents pointed out, has been continued by Morris Udall during his term as the Chair of the House Interior and Insular Affairs Committee.

THE IMPORTANCE OF GOOD LOBBYING

Respondents viewed the quality of the legislative proposal and effectively lobbying it as very important to the development of a sympathetic orientation to Indian interests. Respondents who explicitly mentioned this source of influence (54.4 percent) had in mind several related attributes of policy development.

First, as much as possible, the legislation should be grounded in Indian law—the treaties, statutes, and court decisions and the constitutional mandate on Indian affairs. The "merits of the case" argument thus refers to making policy proposals that are tied to meeting trust responsibility obligations. The Maine land settlement, for example, originated with the discovery, from under an old Passamaquoddy woman's bed in 1957, of a treaty signed in 1794. The treaty implied that the state of Maine had illegally appropriated Indian lands in violation of the 1790 Intercourse Acts. Eventually, the courts upheld this view and the Passamaquoddy-Penobscot claims were settled in 1980. In the same way, the 1978 legislation protecting the religious rights of Indians or their right to decide the welfare of Indian children was based on the "merits of the case."

A second characteristic of good proposal writing, especially if the request cannot be attached to existing laws, is to develop a rationale based in research and, if possible, tied to documentation that proves or suggests a link between some previous act of Congress and some present-day consequence that is economically, politically, or morally unacceptable to decision makers. Restoration legislation that rescinds termination acts or recognizes the existence of a tribe is such an example. Thus, Congress' decision to restore the Menominee to tribal status centered on evidence that termination had caused poverty and economic regression. Similarly, other tribes, like the Cow Creek Bank of the Umpqua and Siletz Tribes of Oregon and the Modoc, Wyandotte, Peoria, and Ottawa of Oklahoma, may be restored to federal recognition after meeting criteria that include proving their tribal identities. Washington, D.C., firms representing Indian tribes seeking restoration and recognition in Congress pride themselves on the credibility and trustworthiness of their research and may tend to attribute their success largely to this type of work.

Furthermore, once legislation is developed, the proposal must be lobbied well. During the 1970s, Indians were perceived as being "much better with briefcases than with tomahawks." Thus, one respondent comments on the Menominee legislation as follows:

Much is due to the Menominee leadership, in particular, Ada Deer, who formed an organization and got community support for restoration. The case had to be put together for Congress. There was not real opposition that I can recall. [There was opposition from lake-side property owners who were not Indians but it did not substantially affect the legislation.] It built on the Nixon message and demonstrated that Indians themselves could do it. The Menominee did a good job of organizing. They got the support of Indian organizations and the Administration and Congress. They did their homework and politicking. They demonstrated how the economic and social situation had deteriorated from 1954 to 1973. It made for a compelling case—the number of people on welfare and the poverty. They also had the Wisconsin delegation [and John Mitchell's, then Attorney General] support. Much of the politicking was accomplished through personal contact.

Effective lobbying by Indians was a very important source of their influence on congressional policy development processes in the seventies. For one thing, Indian lobbying often used traditional imagery—clothing, music, food, and ritual—in the knowledge that Congress and the public tend to associate this imagery with real Indianness. For another, colorful Indian lobbyists provided excellent photo opportunities. Indian lobbying that sought to exploit America's image of the Indian in these respects was thus widely perceived to have positively contributed to the successful representation of Indian policy interests. A composite narrative from several respondents serves to illustrate this point:

By and large, though, if they play their cards right and don't wear three-piece suits, Indians get a hell of a good reception in this town. Especially if they come as traditional native people, are respectful, and give congressmen a good photo opportunity. There's a deep, large reservoir of good will here, at least that's been my experience. It gives them a 40 percent advantage over any other group, if they want it. And, there are many who play it like consummate geniuses....

They're unique. Usually on the Hill you see the same damn people—whether men or women—in blue suits or grey—they're all interchangeable. But then—every now and then—you'll see some Indians and it's a little different. Their appearance shows, first, that they are not the standard hired gun. And, two, it carries with it American history. When they have something to say, senators, congressmen, and staff are very interested in talking to them, more so than to just a lobbyist, who, even if he's wearing a pearl button shirt, sporting a stetson, and his name on the back of his belt, might still be from Yale.... You have three categories of them, almost three stereotypes: the Peter MacDonald Indians are usually dressed like a business person. They are urbane, refined, sophisticated in the ways of the non-Indian world. But, they are always well-listened to because they have an Indian background; they're not Apple Indians (red on the outside, white on the inside). They grew up on the reservation and they have made it in the other world. The few people who realize what this means know how difficult that is to do. Second, you have the ones who are insecure and lack sophistication and education. Mostly, they don't want to turn down a chance to go to Washington. The third group is the majority. They know what they're after and won't get lost pursuing it. They have a sense of mission, dedication. They don't get sidetracked with the Committees' problems.

They look right through the guy when he starts that song and dance and, after he is through, say, "our people are starving on the reservations, what are you going to do about it?"

... On the other hand, the younger, more educated, Indians will be [expletive deleted] if *they're* gonna act like traditional Indians—theirs is the "these are our rights and your responsibility" attitude. And, they *will* wear the three-piece suit and take the congressman to an expensive dinner, and talk oil prices, and may not be as effective. Maybe.

On these occasions, Indians sparked memories of themselves as "noble savages" as well as feelings of guilt about the treatment of Indians historically. Respondents seemed to think that the combination of romantic imagery and guilt was especially effective, in the seventies, in predisposing Congress to consider Indian views more generously than is true for politically powerless minorities as a rule.

An important caveat to the impression that Indians were therefore consummate lobbyists is found in the view of respondents that Indians have not had an easy time establishing their trustworthiness or in following the protocol of proposal development, two other important characteristics of policy development. For example, one group of Indian constituents is said to have told their congressman that they wanted a certain piece of land returned to them for religious purposes. According to accounts, this member interceded in their behalf only to watch the tribe use the property to set up a bingo game. The member's disillusionment with his Indian constituency is supposed to be the reason that he currently opposes Indian interests. Similarly, Indian lobbyists are criticized for not following protocol—for wanting to see members on short notice, for refusing to deal with staff, or for questioning the good will and intentions of legislators.

To a certain extent, however, the unwillingness of Indian lobbyists to sometimes observe the polite forms of congressional discourse and interaction is a deliberate attempt to focus attention on questions of racism and discrimination. Obviously, these are subjects that often lead to confrontation and divisiveness in minority-nonminority relations. Generally, however, Indians are perceived to have acquitted themselves well even on these fronts.

APPROPRIATIONS, CONGRESSIONAL DELEGATIONS, AND COMMITTEE STAFF

Other sources of congressional influence on Indian policy development that helped establish self-determination policies in Congress are: appropriations processes, local congressional delegations, and committee staff.

Appropriations committee decisions—deciding to allocate funds, or how much—are important to Indian policy development because Indian programs are almost entirely a function of federal spending. Their importance is captured in the following comment by respondents:

The name of the game, though, in Indian affairs is appropriations. You have to deal with this committee and they pass substantive legislation all the time. ...The 1871 Appropriations Act, for example, said, "this money...shall not be used for making treaties." So, there were no more treaties...appropriations are always important. Nothing goes anywhere without it. There's a lot of legislation which goes through any committee which gets bogged down in the subcommittees. There are fights over jurisdiction. So what you do is tag on a lot of legislation as amendments to appropriations bills. These might occasionally get knocked at on a point of order, but the trick is that you can always get Rules to suspend the rules of order and go ahead and deal with it....Indian affairs gets dealt with this way, like any other.

The importance of appropriations is also illustrated by the fact that Sidney Yates, who was the only member of the AIPRC who was not on an Indian committee, was then chair of the House Interior's Subcommittee on Appropriations for Indian affairs.

Respondents suggested that, for most of the seventies, appropriations decisions were generally favorable to Indian interests. The caveat—that appropriations committees are not supposed to make substantive policy decisions—is a fine distinction that is often obscured by the fact that policy requires adequate funding in order to accomplish its goal. Thus, respondents probably did not mention appropriations more often because their tendency was to view appropriations as automatically important, especially to policy implementation. Nonetheless, it is also true that substantive policy decisions are typically justified for political, economic, and philosophical reasons that are different from those considered in making appropriations decisions.

Similarly, the support of congressional delegations for policies that will affect Indian and non-Indian interests in a specific political jurisdiction constitutes a much more important dimension of Indian policy development than the lay public generally is aware is true. Thus, respondents perceived local delegations to have been supportive of Indian interests in the seventies. Menominee restoration efforts, for example, were supported by Wisconsin's congressional delegation very early on.

Restoration and recognition legislation is widely regarded as needing the backing of local delegations in order to succeed. Indeed, policy specialists saw the support of local delegations as required: "The rule of thumb, in all the twenty-five years I've been in the business," as one respondent put it, "is that no legislation affecting a specific tribe will clear Congress unless the two senators and the congressmen involved from the districts agree that it will pass." Although "the rule is not honored 100 percent of the time anymore," the Interior Committee's desire to serve all of its constituencies well is a norm that encourages developing only those proposals that have the local delegation's approval.

In fact, the support of local delegations on tribal-specific issues reflects a pervasive value for bipartisanship, or nonpartisanship, in Indian affairs and in the Indian committees as well. One reason for nonpartisanship in Indian affairs is, as we have seen, a normative value for not being perceived as anti-Indian which, in turn, reflects the cultural belief that Indians are special, unique, the first Americans. A second reason for bipartisanship speaks to the reality that Indian policy development is typically low profile, that is, involving complex legal questions and administrative matters. Thus, the policy community involved in legislation is usually small in number and highly specialized, making agreement much easier to achieve.

Finally, Indian committee staff are widely perceived as important to the successful development of Indian legislation. They also were probably not cited more often than they were because, like appropriations and local delegation support, staff are automatically understood, by insiders, to be important to the policy-making process. During the seventies, therefore, Indian committee staff were much more likely to be Indian advocates than not. Thus, staffers like Forest Gerard and Frank Ducheneaux did a great deal to provide Indians with access to Congress, to ensure that their views were heard, and in teaching them the tactics of effective lobbying. On the other hand, when committee staff are not favorably disposed toward Indian interests, they can do significant harm. Jim Gambell, staff for Indian affairs under Wayne Aspinall, was such an example, and a proponent of termination.

Hiring policies may thus play a prominent role in determining the chance that Indian policy preferences will succeed. No doubt this is one reason that Indians and other minorities have consistently defended affirmative action policies. For example, Indians have successfully defended preferential hiring policies in the BIA. Forest Gerard also served as Assistant Secretary of Interior for Indian Affairs for a brief time in 1977.

Despite the wide variety of forces that converged in the 1970s to enable the furtherance of Indian policy goals, their momentum did not proceed entirely unchecked. Toward the end of the decade, the Congress slowed its advocacy for Indian causes with a backlash of legislation aimed at stopping the pro-Indian policy shift.

THE CONGRESSIONAL BACKLASH IN INDIAN AFFAIRS

Mention of the backlash, which emerged full-blown after 1977, and that refers to the Congress' unwillingness to go along with the pro-Indian momentum, at least for a brief time, is the only major factor that respondents saw as detrimental to the establishment of the pro-Indian shift. Thus, 53 percent of them indicated that, by 1980, the backlash had slowed down the change that was taking place. Nevertheless, it did not stop the enactment of legislation favorable to Indian interests. Thus, the occurrence of the backlash is most relevant for what it can tell us about the limits to congressional advocacy.

The backlash began with a bang. In 1978 alone, eleven bills were introduced into the 95th Congress that had the specific intention of stripping Indian rights to the control of their lands and resources. So unmistakable was the attack on Indian rights that Representative Teno Roncalio from Wyoming, then chair of the House Indian Subcommittee, was moved to comment, "It's a difficult time, I haven't seen this much anti-Indian legislation in eight years." The most notorious of these bills, and the one that drew the most media attention and negative response from the Indian community, was introduced by Representative John E. Cunningham (R-Washington).

It will be recalled that Washington State had lost the court battle over Indian fishing rights and that Cunningham had replaced Lloyd Meeds in the House. Cunningham's bill, euphemistically entitled "The Native American Opportunity Act," would have provided for the abrogation of all existing treaties between the tribes and federal government; abolished the BIA; terminated the trust responsibility; abolished hunting and fishing rights; and made all Indians subject to federal, state, and local fish and game regulations. The heart of the bill would have required transferring tribal property to individual adult Indians and liquidation of trust titles held in common, much the same principle that had guided the development of allotment legislation in 1887.[3]

In addition, Cunningham's rationale for the legislation emphasized freeing the Indians from oppressive interference, allowing them to control their own resources. This was almost exactly the same justification that was used by Arthur Watkins twenty-six years earlier, in developing termination legislation. Other abrogation or anti-Indian legislation, some of it introduced by Meeds himself, urged giving the states authority over the tribes on all jurisdictional matters.

The debate on the abrogation legislation was dramatic. Congressmen grandstanded that Indians had had enough, whereas 2,800 Indians, representing seventy tribes, marched to Washington, in July 1978, to protest these actions. Significantly, nothing came of the abrogation legislation. It was not enacted because, unlike the momentum it was intended to rescind, it was too extreme, too controversial, and too visible.

The legislation was too extreme because it called for unilaterally terminating the trust relationship, an action that, although technically legal, was impossible given what we know about the constitutional mandate in Indian affairs. It was too controversial because Indians mobilized immediately and effectively against it, once again raising the spectre of Indian activism that had haunted the federal government through the early seventies. Finally, it was too visible because, whereas Indian affairs are typically legislated by experts and with little interest from other members of Congress or the public, abrogation legislation was sweeping in scope and affected the interests of too many publics to be feasible. Arguably, Indian legislation has thus actually benefited from the reality that few know about, or care, what happens in a policy area that benefits so few people and is so legally and morally complex in substance.

What the abrogation legislation did accomplish, therefore, was to provide Congress with an opportunity to ventilate the feelings of many that the Indians had gained too much at the expense of non-Indians. The backlash happened, in other words, because the accumulation of Indian victories finally struck non-Indians as unfair. On land-related issues alone, since 1970, Indians had won major settlements in Alaska and Maine and the Ute Mountain Utes were suing for four million acres in Utah (they won, in 1986). Smaller claims of large symbolic importance had been won by the Pueblo and the Yakima. Moreover, the Boldt decision, restoring fishing rights to Washington's Indians, threatened to set a precedent upholding treaty rights in other states.

In addition, at the time of the backlash, Congress was also besieged with eastern Indian claims. Hence, the Wampanoag Tribe of Mashpee, Cape Cod, was claiming the town of Mashpee for 17,000 acres. The Narraganset were claiming 3,200 acres in Charlestown, Rhode Island; the Schaghticoke of Connecticut, 1,300 acres; and the Western Pequot, 1,000 acres. In New York State, the Oneida were claiming 300,000 acres, and the Mohawk, 14,000 acres. Although this list does not exhaust the number of claims being filed or pending legislation, it does illustrate why Congress may have felt that its advocacy for Indian rights had got out of control. Again, it is important to emphasize that in thus extending the scope of Indian affairs to previously unaffected publics, Indian issues became more visible and more controversial. Accordingly, eastern liberals who had previously supported (western) Indian causes withdrew their support or chose to remain silent in view of the possible consequences for their own constituencies.

Many non-Indians responded to Indian policy victories by organizing groups like Montanans Against Discrimination (MAD) and the Interstate Congress for Equal Rights and Responsibilities (ICERR), which at one point had 10,000 members in 17 states. They wrote letters, lobbied their members of Congress, and often found a sympathetic audience. Nevertheless, they did not succeed in reversing the policy and attitudinal changes that occurred in the seventies. Significantly, neither organization is presently in existence, although new anti-Indian organizations and campaigns have recently cropped up in response to Minnesota Indian successes in protecting their hunting and fishing rights.

It is also true that extremist organizations, like the ICERR, rely on blatantly racist sentiments and therefore are not as likely to attract as much support as more moderate groups might. Nevertheless, these organizations do attract attention with sensationalistic propaganda, such as "Treaty Beer," which is being sold to raise funds to fight Indian treaty rights. Indians, however, are not likely to underestimate the impact of anti-Indian rights organizations and have recently developed educational strategies intended to inform the public about their treaty rights, which are poorly understood by non-Indians. The "Honor" Coalition presently being formed in Minnesota is an example of the Indian's efforts to educate the public.

In 1978, however, the Supreme Court did rule, in *Oliphant v. Suquamish Indian Tribe*, that the tribes did not have criminal jurisdiction over non-Indians who commit crimes on the reservation. The victory for non-Indians was doubly significant in that the court held that there are "inherent limitations" on tribal sovereignty stemming from the fact that tribes are geographical units within the United States. The decision was thus a victory for non-Indian interests and continues to fuel anti-Indian hopes that the tribes can be prevented from further extending their sovereign powers to non-Indians.

In the meantime, the 95th Congress was exhibiting other symptoms of the backlash. It became impossible to find anyone who would chair the Indian committees. Thus, as one respondent put it:

The result was to kill the House Subcommittee. Nobody would be persuaded to chair it, except the Guam and Virgin Islands representatives. It was a permanent demise. The same thing for the Senate—they had to reorganize and establish an ad hoc [in lieu of a permanent] Indian Committee. . . . Congress has become very, very cautious about handling Indian legislation. It's become controversial now . . . since Indians have become more assertive—in bingo, on tax immunity, the smoke shops—they have high visibility. So, any proposal congressmen introduce on these things is noticed.

Morris Udall, in effect, saved a place for Indian policy in the House by retaining Frank Ducheneaux as a special assistant on Indian affairs to the House Interior and Insular Affairs Committee, of which Udall is the chair. Moreover, the Senate Committee on Indian Affairs was made permanent in 1984, after the backlash had died down.

Obviously, Indian access to Congress remains intact. The observation that Indian policy has become more visible and that members of Congress are therefore more cautious about it than they were in the early seventies is important, however. It suggests that as Indians have gained influence they have also had to pay a price. Thus, in acquiring influence over Indian affairs, Indian interests have come more and more to resemble conventional interest groups. Increasingly, that is, Indian groups have come to behave with moderation and to accept compromises that in a more activist era were unnecessary.

The favorable climate for Indian interests created in the seventies continues, as is evidenced by legislation enacted after 1978. In the domain of social welfare policy, for example, contract schools continue to grow in number, ensuring Indian control over tribal educational programs. Moreover, attempts to pass legislation that would force the tribes to contract before they are ready have been defeated, thereby protecting the educational rights of Indian children. Similarly, Indian child welfare legislation, first enacted in 1978, continues to favor Indian control despite enormous opposition to the implementation of these programs from local authorities. Finally, Indian health legislation has survived presidential vetoes and the government's unwillingness to adequately fund them.

With respect to land-related issues, land claims settlements have continued to be made to numerous tribes, among them: the Seminole and Miccosukee, the Paiute and Shoshone, the Ute Mountain Ute, the Moapa, the Pueblo de Cochiti, and the Narragansett, to name a few. In addition, the Indian Tribal Governmental Tax Status Act of 1983 gives Indians the same rights as other governments to raise revenues and save money and the Indian Mineral Development Act of 1982 allows the tribes to enter into joint ventures on energy development projects. These measures enable Indian tribes to control their own development and to profit from their decisions.

Thus, the backlash did not succeed in reversing Congress' self-determination orientation toward Indian policy development. What it did was to make it a little harder to obtain support for Indian causes and more difficult to introduce innovative and comprehensive legislation of the omnibus type of the seventies. The backlash was also the politician's way of reigning in the momentum toward greater sovereignty for Indian tribes, and was therefore one last attempt to reassert the federal government's plenary authority over Indian affairs.

Finally, it remains to be seen how much farther along the road toward political sovereignty the tribes will travel. The question of political status has by no means been resolved. Perhaps the most significant accomplishment of the policy-making era of the seventies, then, was to place this question at the center of federal-Indian relations in such a way that it is not likely to disappear. Thus, modern perceptions of sovereignty have become deeply rooted in Congress' approach to Indian policy-making and in the consciousness of contemporary advocates, each of whom, in their own way, equate Indian sovereignty with greater control over policies and programs.

Nevertheless, the case for the Indians' new political clout should not be overstated. The abrogation legislation was sincerely intended to respond to non-Indian concerns and to give voice to the public interest. Furthermore, Indians remain low men on the political totem pole and it is not at all certain they will develop the necessary electoral strategies suggested by this study to maximize their influence on policy development. Chapters 7 and 8 deal with the subject of Indian political power.

NOTES

1. The following quote by an early agent of the Indian department, as the BIA was known then, describes sentiments about the BIA that have remained current:

The derangements in the fiscal affairs of the Indian Department are in the extreme. One would think that appropriations had been handled with a pitchfork.... And these derangements are only with regard to the North. How the South and West stand, it is impossible to say. But there is a screw loose in the public machinery somewhere. (Schoolcraft, quoted in Prucha, 1962, p. 59)

2. It is apparently a commonly held belief that presidential candidates must not be perceived as anti-Indian. The following quote describes how this principle worked to refurbish Senator Henry Jackson's image on Indian affairs and, by the same token, to advance Indian interests. Fenno (1973, p. 179) made the complementary observation that Jackson's "interests" lay "elsewhere" than in making a career in the Senate.

Along about then (1968) Jackson began looking at the national scene and saw Indian affairs was his blind spot.... Jackson became presidential, and presidential candidates are never anti-Indian.... This sold him on the idea of bringing in new [pro-Indian] people. ...Thus, the climate began shifting in the Senate.... We began to improve Jackson's image. We got another concurrent resolution [in the Senate only] repudiating termination. It was a signal to Indians that maybe things were changing. We began modifying legislation Congress had set forward and which had been around a long time.... We looked for omnibus legislation to handle.... The final chapter will show he served Native Americans well.... Although he didn't think of himself as an Indian advocate, it was his own deep values that moved him to accept arguments like self-determination.

3. For a discussion of this and other aspects of the backlash see Kellogg (1978, pp. 24–30); *National Journal* (1978, pp. 1353–1355); *Congressional Quarterly* (1978, pp. 3385–3388). These are excellent accounts of the popular response to issues raised by the backlash.

7

The Indian Influence on Policy Development in the 1970s

The findings of this study strongly suggest that Indians themselves played a prominent role in the federal government's shift toward a pro-Indian policy development perspective. This chapter shows how the Indians—acting as individual policy entrepreneurs, in groups, and through non-Indian advocates—contributed to the idea that they should represent themselves on policy matters.

How did the Indians come to influence the course of Indian affairs? As we have seen, there is little in the historical record to indicate that Indians had ever been influential in their own behalf.

Indian influence was very importantly a product of the civil rights era of the 1960s. Thus, public opinion supportive of equal rights and equal opportunity for American racial and ethnic minorities helped create a climate of opinion sympathetic to Indian demands for freedom and equality. The advocates of a pro-Indian policy orientation were able to exploit this climate and therefore to take advantage of increased federal spending and other factors to bring about changes in accord with their own preferences. Namely, they composed a political agenda focusing on the protection and restoration of treaty rights, renewed commitment to the trust responsibility, and greater control over the direction and management of their own internal affairs. As Table 7.1

Table 7.1
Sources of Indian and Friend of Indian Influence on Indian Policy Development

Source	Percent of Respondents[a] ($\underline{N}$ = 66)	Number of Mentions[b] (Times Mentioned)	
		1 and 2	3 or More
Formal Indian organizations	72.7	57	38
Indian tribes	65.2	40	47
Washington representatives (lobbies)	62.1	32	47
Indians as unable to plan; lacking the resources to manage own affairs	57.6	39	14
Indian movement/red power	51.5	45	9
Tribal leadership	51.5	44	6
Indian savvy	43.9	33	23
Indian militancy	43.9	35	14
Indians inside government	42.4	32	9
Non-Indian advocates inside government	42.4	27	23

[a]The percentage indicated refers only to those respondents who mentioned the source. Percentages do not total 100 percent because respondents who do not mention the source are not counted.

[b]The number of times mentioned is based on how many times during an interview the source was mentioned. Number of mentions suggests the importance of the source in the perception of the respondent(s).

shows, the Indian political agenda was realized in five ways: through social movement activism; through political savvy in using the mechanisms of governmental institutions to advantage; through tribal leadership initiatives; through policy entrepreneurship by individuals inside and outside of government; and by "friends of the Indian"—historical allies, like the Association on American Indian Affairs (AAIA), and paid lobbyists.

RED POWER AND SOCIAL MOVEMENT ORGANIZATIONS

One way in which the impact of the civil rights era was felt in Indian affairs was in the formation of an Indian social movement that had its contemporary counterparts in the "Black Power" and "Brown Power" movements of the sixties.[1] Red Power activism drew media attention and helped to publicize the plight of the Indian through dramatic confrontations—sit-ins, takeovers, and demonstrations—with official authorities.

Respondents seemed to feel that, at least between 1968 and 1972, Indian collective actions served a useful purpose. After 1972, with the takeover of the Bureau of Indian Affairs (BIA) building in Washington, D.C., support for Indian militancy declined. By then, however, Indian activists had made their rejection of BIA paternalism well-known and had contributed to developing a new political agenda on treaty rights, Indian sovereignty, and Indian control.

The contemporary Indian movement began in Chicago, in 1961, at a conference convened under the auspices of the National Congress of American Indians (NCAI) and anthropologist Sol Tax. It brought together 420 Indians from sixty-seven tribes, most of them college students or recent graduates (Hertzberg, 1971). The Chicago conference produced a "Declaration of Indian Purpose," which affirmed the rights of Indians to preserve their cultural and spiritual identities and to control their own destinies (Josephy, 1971). Most importantly, it called on Indians to set aside tribal differences in the interests of an Indian policy that would benefit all of them (Josephy, 1971). This call to a new pan-Indianism was accompanied by a commitment to a collective actions strategy that would accomplish two purposes: force official authorities to give in to Indian demands and create public sympathy for the victimization of the Indians.

Many of the young Indians present at the conference went on to form the National Indian Youth Council (NIYC), in August of 1961. The NIYC was known for its militant activism and figures prominently in the collective actions of the sixties, among them the occupation of Alcatraz Island and other federal properties (Hertzberg, 1971; Svensson, 1973).[2]

The occupation of the abandoned federal penitentiary at Alcatraz, in November of 1969, was an event of lasting significance for Indian policy development. Seventy-eight Indians, calling themselves "Indians of All Tribes," took up residence at Alcatraz under an 1868 Treaty with the Sioux that gave the Indians the right to surplus federal properties. Several deaths, and the hardships they endured, drew extensive media attention as well as sustained involvement by officials of the Nixon administration, who played an important role in bringing about a settlement. By the time the occupation ended, in 1971, the Indians' resistance made them into a "symbol of freedom" (Josephy, 1984, p. 230). Even more importantly, their willingness to risk their lives captured public sympathy and focused attention on treaty rights.

Alcatraz was a watershed of the Indian Movement but served to catalyze numerous other collective actions that kept public attention on the Indian political agenda. Dozens of other takeovers followed the occupation of Alcatraz. Among some of the more prominent were: the occupation of Ft. Lawton in Seattle (1970); attempts to occupy BIA offices in Chicago, Minneapolis, Philadelphia, Cleveland, Los Angeles, Albuquerque, Littleton, Colorado, and Alameda, California; the Pomo and Pit River Indian occupation of former tribal lands in northern California; Sioux demonstrations at Mt. Rushmore in the Black Hills of South Dakota; the Wisconsin Chippewa occupation of a Coast Guard station; an attempt by the New York Tuscarora to eject whites from their reservations; and an attempt to occupy Ellis Island (*New York Times Index*, 1969–1972).[3]

Indian activism was spurred on by the "fish-ins" of Washington State that began in 1964 and continued until 1974, when the Boldt decision established the Indians' treaty rights to fish independently of state statutes that applied to non-Indians. The early fish-ins, and even those occurring today in Wisconsin and Minnesota, were often violent confrontations between the Indians, non-Indians, and state officials. Importantly, they were accompanied by a great deal of publicity—media attention that was enhanced by the presence of celebrities like Dick Gregory and Marlon Brando. Significantly, these actions helped to sustain the focus on treaty rights and thus on the development of an Indian political agenda in Washington, D.C.

Much of the social activism of the late sixties and early seventies was led by one organization in particular, the American Indian Movement (AIM). AIM was started, in Minneapolis, as an organization whose purpose was to protect Indians from abuse by the local police. By 1972, however, under the leadership of Dennis Banks and Russell Means, AIM had developed a national agenda. That year, a "Caravan of Broken Treaties" was organized. Its purpose was to cross the United States, from points originating in Los Angeles, San Francisco, and Seattle, in order to present a list of demands claiming treaty rights. The Caravan ended by occupying the offices of the BIA in Washington, D.C., with mixed results. At issue in determining AIM's effectiveness in this instance were questions about the degree of property damage done, and by whom; to what extent Caravan activists were representative of Indians in general; and about the propriety of the Nixon administration's decision to buy off Indian leadership by providing them with $66,650 in Office of Economic Opportunity (OEO) funds to return home.[4]

Indian social activism reached its peak in 1973, with an armed confrontation at Wounded Knee on the Pine Ridge Reservation, in South Dakota, which lasted seventy-one days. The reasons for the occupation were complex, having to do both with the symbolic importance of the site (the scene of a massacre of Sioux Indians by U.S. forces in 1890) and with an attempt to replace tribal leadership with AIM activists. Media coverage extensively publicized the event, which included attempts by Nixon administration officials to end the siege.[5]

Respondents for this study agreed that, after the takeover of the BIA and Wounded Knee, support for the Indians noticeably eroded. Thus, AIM's activities were severely curtailed. Its leadership was imprisoned or went into hiding to avoid arrest. In Washington, the Nixon administration's support for an Indian agenda waned—Harrison Loesch, then Assistant Secretary of Interior, and an influential advocate for Indian causes, for example, became opposed to further concessions. The general impression was that Indians had gone too far. The feeling was, not only that the militancy had gotten out of hand, but that Indians were not being reasonable or responsive with respect to solutions proposed by the administration.

After 1974, AIM revived as the International Indian Treaty Council, now committed to taking its battle for Indian sovereignty into the international arena. They were accorded nongovernmental organization status by the United Nations and meet periodically on different Indian reservations. AIM's activism is currently confined to an encampment in the Black Hills, Yellow Thunder, whose purpose is to protest a monetary settlement to the Sioux for the Black Hills, and to sporadic appearances in protest of the Navajo-Hopi relocation legislation or to energy development projects.

Indian social movement activism served the very important purpose of focusing public attention on the Indian political agenda at a time when both the society and elected officials were included to view minority causes with sympathy and a great deal of interest. Nevertheless, the effectiveness of the social movement organizations was not the result of a systematic or planned effort to achieve Indian policy goals, in other words, of revolution or elections. Thus, social movement activism has traditionally played a role in American politics by forcing attention on the needs and concerns of the politically powerless. In the 1960s and early 1970s, movement activism focused public sympathy on the Indian plight and forced public officials to respond to Indian demands.

In this century, social activism, as a result of the Great Depression, helped spawn the New Deal and social security legislation. Similarly, civil rights activism in the 1950s and 1960s notably influenced the development of anti-discrimination and affirmative action legislation and welfare rights for the poor. To the extent conditions threatening social organization and stability no longer apply, therefore, Indian political interests have to rely on using electoral system mechanisms to impact the policy agenda. The creation of formal Indian organizations is one way in which policy influence has been achieved through these means.

FORMAL INDIAN ORGANIZATIONS

A significant number of respondents (72.7 percent) cited the positive influence of Indian organizations on policy development in the 1970s. By Indian organizations respondents meant those formal interest groups that led issue-specific fights, like the Alaska Federation of Natives in the case of the Alaska Claims Act, or the Passamaquoddy and Penobscot Tribes, in the Maine Settlement Act; or they were referring to formal Indian organizations, like the National Tribal Chairman's Association (NTCA) or the NCAI, which had national constituencies and took positions on most of the major legislation of the seventies.

Historically, there were very few Indian organizations with a pan-Indian agenda. That of the defunct Society of American Indians, for example, had been to find ways to assimilate into American society, not to establish a separate political status through the trust relationship.[6] Thus, the NCAI was founded, in 1944, by World War II and Korean War veterans, for anyone of Indian ancestry. In contrast, the NTCA, created in 1971, limited membership to tribal leadership. The NCAI's purpose was to give voice to Indian policy interests by initiating and promoting a pro-Indian agenda and by actively opposing termination (LaCourse, 1973; Svensson, 1973). Thus, the NCAI's agenda emphasized protecting treaty rights and preserving the trust relationship by using the electoral system (LaCourse, 1973). Although a basic difference between the NTCA and NCAI is that the former was viewed as an organ of the Nixon administration, both organizations benefited from federal funding and each was an important source of Indian leadership in legislative battles.

The Americans for Indian Opportunity (AIO) also benefited from War on Poverty funding. Under LaDonna Harris' leadership, it continues the Indian organizational tradition of watch-dogging legislation and exerting influence on the federal agenda (AIO Annual Reports, 1979–1984; Americans for Indian Opportunity, 1971). The AIO also created the Native American Legal Defense and Education Fund (NALDEF), which acts to advance Indian legal and educational policies.

Interestingly, the Native American Political Action Coalition (NAPAC), founded in 1982, may be the prototype of a new Indian organization whose purpose will be to develop local Indian constituencies in the conventional sense. Thus, although NAPAC itself has apparently not had much success in bringing Indians to the electoral process through voter education and registration campaigns or in lobbying state legislatures, the success of Indian interest groups in the seventies argues for more formal political organizations.

Frequently criticized by respondents for their tendency to engage in internecine conflicts, to become fragmented with respect to their agreement about goals and strategies, or for their inability to manage internal planning processes well, national Indian organizations nevertheless came through when the going got rough. Thus, when policy specialists described the effectiveness of formal Indian organizations, they were emphasizing their representativeness, and especially their ability to mobilize Indian opinion and support across the country on very short notice. Therefore, the national organizations were perceived as effective because of their capability to threaten actions that might create public or political situations that government officials tend to view as embarrassing or otherwise untenable. The public demonstrations of the seventies are an example of this point.

In addition to focusing public attention on the need for justice in Indian affairs, Indian conventions provided a forum for developing an Indian position on the issues and a meeting ground for exchanges with public officials, such as those that occurred during the presidential campaigns of 1968 and 1972. Thus, they also created a place for the expression of urban Indian interests, forging a closer alliance between divergent tribal groups and the cities. In this endeavor, national organizations obviously did not act alone. Indian tribes played a central role in developing the political agenda and in bringing about the policy successes of the seventies.

INDIAN TRIBES AND TRIBAL LEADERSHIP

Respondents (65.2 percent) viewed Indian tribes, and tribal leadership specifically (51.5 percent), as important sources of influence on policy development during the seventies. Thus, much of the successful land claims legislation of the decade, from Blue Lake to Maine, benefited from the tenacious efforts of individual tribes to assert treaty rights. The 1975 Submarginal Lands Act Amendment, for example, returned land in trust to tribes who had been promised it in 1933, forty-two years earlier. John Stevens, of the Passamaquoddy, almost single-handedly initiated the momentum for the Maine Settlement of 1980, in 1965. And Ada Deer, for awhile Chairperson of the Menominee Tribe, was instrumental in bringing about the Menominee Restoration Act of 1973. Similarly, on issues of economic growth, the leadership of Peter MacDonald, of the Navajo Tribe, was and still is the focus of national and international attention.

One reason for their influence—which today manifests itself in decisions being made about the economic development of reservations, in water rights negotiations, and on hunting and fishing rights, as well as land issues—is that the tribes are key players in the federal-Indian relationship. Their semisovereign status, which was given fresh recognition during the 1970s, thus places them in the constitutional system of intergovernmental relations. These are complicated relationships because the Indians have won important court decisions affirming their rights to govern themselves and to assert jurisdiction over tribal matters and over land, water, and other natural resources. Thus, especially with respect to civil jurisdiction—zoning, taxation, gambling—and natural resource use and development, tribal authority frequently conflicts with the authority claimed by states and local governments. One result of the conflict has been to provide fodder for the courts and an ongoing agenda for Congress.

Another reason for tribal influence is the tribal-specific nature of much Indian legislation. Thus, legislation is frequently intended to benefit or solve a problem belonging to a particular tribe. For example, much Indian policy deals with the settlement, disposition, and distribution of government funds awarded to the tribes by the courts for the redress of treaty violations. Other legislation may deal with land sales, transfers, exchanges, or conveyances, leases, mineral and water rights, putting lands in trust or even concession fee contracts in the national parks. In another example, in 1974, the northern Cheyenne successfully sought the cancellation of their coal leases because the leases had not been managed in their best interests by the BIA. There has been other legislation that attempts to rectify violations of tribal rights by the agencies of the federal government's trusteeship.

Tribal influence during the seventies also made itself felt through the Council of Energy Resource Tribes (CERT). Formed in 1975, the council was led by Peter MacDonald and the leaders of twenty-two other tribes. Its purpose was to further the political clout of energy resource owning tribes. CERT has been a source of controversy: partly because most tribes are not energy-rich in the same way, and the organization is therefore viewed as unrepresentative of Indian interests, and partly because of its tactics. In 1977, for example, CERT met with representatives of OPEC to discuss possible collaborations. As a result, the federal government pledged $200,000 of BIA and economic development administration grant money to open a D.C. office for the council and, one year later, another $2 million for training, research, and a Denver office. Nevertheless, as this example illustrates, CERT has been effective. Among other things, the council has gotten Congress to exempt the tribes from the Oil Windfall Profits Tax; helped the Jicarilla Apache buy a small oil company; assisted the Crow in winning a coal gasification power plant; and won a right-of-way for the Alaska pipeline across the Navajo Reservation.

For these reasons, CERT has also been criticized for placing pro-development over traditional values. This is a criticism worth noting because it points up a source of basic conflict between traditional and progressive values in Indian country. Specifically, there is concern that development may conflict with, or undermine, traditional spiritual, religious, or cultural values. The ambivalence with which economic development is viewed was often noted by policy specialists who think that divisiveness with respect to progress may undercut the ability of Indians to effectively pursue their future policy objectives. One respondent addressed the question this way:

Indian political sophistication has grown. It is only impeded when tradition-alism—wanting to go back to the "old ways" gets in the way. Unanimity and consensus are nice things and maybe they worked then but they don't work now. A tribal council can't meet and not decide and then meet again later to talk about it and on and on like that when an oil company is breathing down their necks. You know decisions don't get made that way. In that day and age, maybe. But today, like it or not, they have to deal with corporations, states, administration, and Congress and these decisions have to be made now.

Many people who write about Indian affairs acknowledge the centrality of Indian values for understanding tribal attitudes and behaviors. Some have tried to identify Indian personality types, whereas others have tried to describe an Indian way (Forbes, 1981; Josephy, 1984; Spindler and Spindler, 1978; Svensson, 1973). Vine Deloria characterized the progressive versus traditional dichotomy in terms that perhaps come closest to what respondents mean.

Deloria described traditionalists as tribal members who can trace their ancestry, who live in the remotest parts of a reservation, who follow traditional social and religious custom, and who speak an Indian language.[7] In fact, language is viewed as the "key to cultural survival" and as a "powerful political weapon" as well as evidence of "real Indianness" (Deloria, 1983, p. 251; Deloria, 1984, p. 233). Finally, traditionalists possess an oral history tradition that enables them to "remember the slightest nuance of meaning in every treaty promise" (Deloria, 1984, p. 243). One respondent put this ability this way:

I don't know anyone who's better at knowing the federal government and how it works. Even old guys, who've never left the reservation and can hardly speak English—I've seen them talk about how the federal government is the Indians' government and always has been. I've always been impressed by the level of knowledge out there.

Consequently, traditionalists are not impressed by the niceties of the law and tend to believe they know their own treaty rights best (Deloria, 1984).

Progressives, on the other hand, are not as culturally distinct a population as the traditionalists. Generally, they are more assimilated; that is, less than full-blooded Indians and more likely to have adopted white middle-class norms and values. Progressives are therefore perceived as more likely to involve themselves with conventional political processes and to be better equipped educationally to do so effectively. Despite this, traditionalists are viewed as possessing a greater moral authority—as culturally superior. These differences contribute to a certain amount of tension in deciding policy matters because progressive values for "getting the job done" expediently conflict with traditional values that are mistrustful and suspicious of "the White man's" promises (Deloria, 1984). Traditionalists, for example, might view the tribal control of federal programs, as authorized by the 1975 self-determination legislation, as merely another approach to termination— as abrogating the trust responsibility to provide free services—while progressives may see the same policy as affirming of tribal sovereignty and the right of the tribe to decide for itself.

Whether or not one considers the influence of traditionalists or progressives more desirable, of course, will depend on one's value orientation. The politics of policy development, however, are such that a willingness to bargain, negotiate, compromise, and take advantage of opportunity requires making trade-offs between value preferences and winning; in other words, getting one's policy preferences enacted. One way in which the dilemmas inherent in the traditional versus progressive dynamic were resolved during the seventies was through the advocacy of "friends of the Indian" and by using paid lobbyists to represent the Indian case.

FRIENDS OF THE INDIAN ORGANIZATIONS AND THE PAID LOBBY

Historically, "friend of the Indian" organizations refer to those that, like the Boston Indian Citizenship Committee (1879), the Women's National Indian Association (1883), or the Lake Mohonk Conference of Friends of the Indian (1883), were founded in order to advocate for Indians against unfair treatment by whites. These organizations tended to be founded, however, by philanthropists who nevertheless believed that Indians should assimilate and become "Americanized," thus ensuring their survival as an ethnically distinct people. They reached the height of their influence between 1880 and 1900, having had the enactment of the allotment legislation of 1887 as their main objective. In their view, of course, severalty meant that the Indians, through the requirement for individual rather than tribal ownership, would be better able to survive in the white world.[8] Thus, their approach to Indian policy was markedly ethnocentric.

Friend of the Indian organizations, like the Indian Rights Association (IRA), for example, were good at mobilizing public opinion and at lobbying the Congress, especially on Indian agent abuses and attempts to dispossess the Indians of their lands (Hagan, 1985). Contemporary friend of the Indian organizations, like the Association on American Indian Affairs (AAIA), use similar tactics—special reports, letters to members of Congress, and editorials, for example—to influence policy development but their outlook on Indian affairs is very different.

Contemporary friend organizations—the Friends Committee on National Legislation is another example—typically support, and help lobby for, Indian-defined policy goals and preferences. They thus resist imposing non-Indian views on Indian affairs policy development. The AAIA, for instance, was instrumental in helping to build an Indian-non-Indian alliance on the child welfare legislation of 1978 and in preparing the data base that was so influential in generating congressional support for the policy. The American Academy of Child Psychiatry assisted in this effort. Another medical organization, the American Academy of Obstetricians and Gynecologists, has been influential in the development of Indian health legislation.

Modern professional associations of this type are viewed as especially credible by policy specialists because they bring recognized expertise to the problem and because their professional status suggests they will be reliable witnesses. Generally, they share one underlying characteristic in common. They are, sometimes for religious reasons—as with the Quakers, or for moral reasons, through their reading of Indian history—committed to the principle that Indians are a sovereign people with treaty rights. Accordingly, they are able to set ethnocentricity aside in favor of self-determination.

Washington lobbies, mentioned by 62.1 percent of respondents as important to Indian policy development in the seventies, are a latter-day phenomena. Interest in taking Indian cases has increased among law firms and other Washington representatives in view of the sizeable fees that may accompany land claims settlements, energy development projects, gaming, and restoration and recognition legislation. A 1970 Library of Congress estimate, for example, put the number of these groups at between 150 and 220, including Friends of the Indian, lobbies for Indian rights and programs, lobbies for augmenting social services to Indians, and intertribal organizations (*The National Journal*, 1970). Appendix C lists for-profit representatives only, as of 1983. Typically, Indian cases involve pitting Indian interests against those of non-Indians, including the states. Thus, Washington representatives have

become increasingly important in deciding questions of tribal jurisdiction, control and economic development.

The perception that Washington representatives are effective is related to two facts. First, they base their legislative proposal development on Indian law and empirical research. And second, they pay
attention to the norms and practices of good lobbying. Both qualities
enhance the credibility of Washington representatives. One respondent
described the effectiveness of the Indian lobby this way: "Preparation
is the key. It isn't just a case of having some Sargeant Shriver type to
go up on the Hill to talk to his buddies. Our success is the result of
first-rate work plus the on-going good relations we have with congressional staff." Another respondent emphasized the importance of credibility as follows:

The Congress has to be confident that we know what we are talking about.
That we are doing our homework and know the surrounding circumstances.
. . . In the more political sense, we answer questions like, "If I'm going to support
this, what's the vote gonna be?" We might say, "If you do it now, you'll lose
it; but, in three weeks. . . . We have to know what's going on. Our credibility
is re-created every time [we] are involved in anything. You can never recover
it if its ever lost."

The use of Washington representatives to advance Indian policy interests has greatly enhanced the ability of Indians to influence the
policy process. Much of the Indians' ability to develop influence, however, depends on the capacity of poorer tribes to acquire the resources
necessary to purchase such influence. The Indians' willingness to use
for-profit lobbyists also depends on reconciling the traditionalist versus
progressive debate in favor of employing conventional mechanisms to
gain influence, as in the following example:

The Lac Courte Oreilles [Chippewa Indians] is a progressive tribe. They are
dealing effectively with the townspeople opposition with an aggressive public
relations campaign. They show how they generate income for the community
of Hayward. They do radio, presentations—focus on the facts. For example,
they show there are more White women on the welfare rolls than Indians. It
makes people sit up and think. They also paid tribal employees in $2 bills to
show local merchants who was making the economic contribution. . . . The Lac
Courte Oreilles have even joined the Chamber of Commerce . . . they've brought
in bingo, too, which is very controversial. But one night they had the townspeople in for a night of bingo and a buffet on the tribe. . . . But I don't see a lot
of other tribes doing the same thing. . . . Maybe they don't have the staff, or
the time, or don't realize the benefit.

Nonetheless, policy specialists clearly agreed that the ability of Indian constituencies and interest groups to use their political savvy in

behalf of their goals made a difference in the seventies and may make even more of a difference in the future. One respondent summed up the importance of developing a conventional perspective on politics this way:

The tribes are getting so sophisticated they have to count on outsider organizations a lot—Washington lobbyists. Indian people have always gone to the Hill because of the federal relationship but now they're going with increased knowledge of how the system works. They know they can't just have a meeting—that they need letters and votes. This is due to the number of American Indians being educated and the number of lawyers. . . . The AIPRC also did wonders. It had forty or fifty Indians up on the Hill all the time. They'd testify all the time and got a feeling for how it works. The Committee staff made a difference too . . . would say, here's how you do it, folks. . . . Then Indian organizations started moving to D.C. with full-time staffs and they started to see results.

In fact, the continued success of a pro-Indian momentum in Indian affairs legislation may depend on the willingness and ability of Indian interests to act as conventional interest groups. Toward this end, Indian tribes and organizations will need to develop their constituencies so that they may also impact policy development through electoral processes—voting, campaigning, or running for public office.

NOTES

1. Josephy (1984) and Steiner (1968) provided excellent accounts of the Indian movement. Josephy (1971) is a collection of documents useful for identifying benchmarks of the movement. In addition, three of Deloria's books provide extensive analysis, from an activist's point of view, of the Indian movement (see Deloria, 1969, 1970, 1974).

2. Hertzberg (1971) also pointed out that the NIYC was responsible for coining phrases that became identified with "Red Power"—for example, "Uncle Tomahawk" and "BIA Indians" to denote those Indians who had "sold out" or become assimilated, and "For a Greater Indian America" to denote the nationalist sentiment that reflected their value for traditional Indian values.

3. Respondents themselves seldom referred to specific events, except for the major events that occurred with the takeover of the BIA building in Washington, D.C., and Wounded Knee. Their references were to sit-ins, fish-ins, occupations, and takeovers in general. The *Times Index* is therefore a useful source for specific times and events.

4. For contrasting points of view on these questions compare Forbes (1973, pp. 75–102) and Taylor (1983, pp. 34–45).

5. Retrospectively, the media vociferously complained about how, in its perception, it had been used and exploited by the militant Indians. The following are particularly fascinating accounts of this view: Hickey (1973, pp. 34–40);

"Cameras Over Here!" (1973, pp. 43–49); "Our Media Blitz" (1973, pp. 221–223); Smith (1973); Schultz (1973, pp. 46–56).

6. The oldest of the pan-Indian organizations was actually a group called the Society of American Indians. Formed in 1911, its purpose was explicitly assimilationist. Unlike the NCAI and the NTCA, its founders and members opposed the BIA because they felt it was helping to perpetuate tribalism and traditional cultures, thus inhibiting assimilation. Never very influential in Indian policy matters, the SAI nevertheless did a great deal to preserve Indian cultures and life-styles but as curiosities rather than as a serious alternative to assimilation into white society. See Hertzberg (1971), whose book, *The Search for An American Indian Identity*, is a case study of the SAI, and Svensson (1973, p. 29).

7. This discussion is based on Deloria (1984, pp. 133–154).

8. This section is based on Prucha (1973, 1978) and Hagan (1985). "Severalty" refers to allotting land in individual parcels rather than to tribal or collective ownership.

8

The Future of American Indian Politics

OVERVIEW OF THE FINDINGS

The historical record of Indian-white relations documents the American government's failure to have properly represented American Indian political interests. Despite the reasonable expectation, therefore, that the contemporary record would be no different, this public policy analysis has shown that the 1970s constituted a genuine turning point in the political fortunes of American Indians. In other words, major legislation enacted after 1968 has, for the most part, incorporated the policy goals and preferences of Indian constituencies and groups. Moreover, the findings of this study suggest that the reasons for this change in the federal government's approach to Indian affairs are varied, complex, and unpredictable. The fact that Indian policy development, like any other, does not therefore follow purely rational processes should not be cause for despair, however. The political nature of Indian policymaking, that is, does not need to detract from the reality that it has been possible to make meaningful public policy. Significantly, Indians themselves have been instrumental in bringing about this new reality.

Indian groups and constituencies, and their advocates, have clearly become important actors in the realm of Indian affairs. Thus, when they make their views and preferences known, public officials are more likely than not to respond by according them the right to participate in formulating the options and substance of formal policy. As well, Indian interests have managed to establish a presence in the Indian affairs policy arena by obtaining a significant degree of control over the administration of programs in Indian country. Thus, overall, the political factors that were responsible for this change in the federal government's approach to Indian policy-making, although they cannot be entirely controlled, are factors that can be anticipated, planned for, and manipulated in important ways. This chapter suggests some of the ways in which the political experience of the 1970s can be used to plan for an Indian political future that will continue to advance a political agenda defined by the Indians themselves. Before proceeding to this task, a brief review of the political lessons learned from this study of Indian affairs should help to refocus our attention on what it is that was gained in the 1970s.

Increased Indian control over, and participation in, the formulation of Indian policy after 1970 was due to the workings of political forces that converged in such a way as to make the institutions of government more responsive to Indian policy views and preferences. In addition, the Indians' own ability to represent their policy interests was significantly enhanced, with the result that legislation enacted during the seventies reflected Indian policy objectives. Historically, of course, Indian views had been suppressed or willfully ignored. Thus, the political accomplishments of the 1970s were especially significant because their end result was to create a new and more powerful role for the expression of Indian views.

Indian policy change was facilitated, first of all, by the creation of a favorable climate of the times, that is, by the emergence of more liberal social attitudes. Thus, public sympathy for minority causes, a significant result of the black civil rights activism of the 1950s and 1960s, played a useful role in advancing an Indian political agenda. Public sympathy for minorities put pressure on elected officials to deal with the nation's poverty, much of which could be found amongst blacks, Hispanics, and American Indians. Public officials responded by enacting new programs.

In addition, Indian activists and policy entrepreneurs were able to use the romantic imagery of the Indian and the contemporary harsh realities of Indian poverty to develop public sympathy for Indian causes, thus ensuring more money for Indian programs and more attention to Indian problems. As well, dramatic Indian confrontations with national and local authorities, and the mass media, created a much larger national audience for telling the Indian story than had ever been true before. The results were beneficial both in terms of generating public support for innovative solutions to old problems and for replacing racist stereotypes of the Indian with alternative, more realistic, views of the modern Indian experience.

Thus, federal spending during the War on Poverty, and Great Society eras directly created opportunities, both on the reservations and in the cities, for the development of new Indian leadership. Educational programs graduated better prepared leadership from institutions of higher learning and the community action programs provided program directors with employment opportunities that had previously been non-existent. Because of the poverty programs, Indians found employment and thus became involved with decisions about the allocation and management of the additional resources poured into Indian country. In its turn, the Indians' enhanced control over the management and development of new programs helped to generate a new confidence that there were, finally, alternatives to the domination of Indian life by the Bureau of Indian Affairs (BIA).

Indians used the new federal programs to create political bases on the reservations and in the cities. Their renewed confidence, and the availability of resources, thus enabled them to form tribal and national organizations whose primary purposes and achievements were to restore balance to the trust relationship by effectively demanding that Indian political goals and preferences be considered in formulating policy goals and developing new programs.

Toward these ends, Indian policy interests were assisted in giving new meaning to the constitutional mandate on Indian affairs by the policy initiatives and administrative support of several presidents, most notably Richard Nixon. Nixon's unprecedented disavowal of the termination ideology, his personal commitment, and his ability to create access to the White House and other institutions of government, was largely responsible for Congress' adoption of a self-determination orientation to the legislation of Indian affairs and thus to the advancement of Indian policy goals. Congress' contribution to the pro-Indian shift in Indian policy development, moreover, was made possible by the aggressive advocacy of Indian committee chairs and their staffs. Congressional leadership made it possible for the representatives of Indian interests to obtain access to policy-making processes and in this way to make their views known in a manner consistent with congressional norms for effective lobbying. Finally, the Indians' own abilities—the effective application of political savvy—made it possible for them either to represent themselves or to employ others who would lobby for them.

This summary of contemporary American Indian policy-making dynamics, and the significant relationships between people, organizations, and events that caused them to work in behalf of Indian political interests during the 1970s, suggests certain conditions that must be met if Indians (and perhaps other minorities) are to remain influential participants in determining the public policies that will enhance the quality of their lives and advance their political agendas. Furthermore, any of these conditions can be met by using the electoral system principles and mechanisms already valued and supported by American society as the best means of accomplishing positive social change. Thus, interest group activity, voter registration and turn-out, electing one's own candidates to public office, pursuing litigative solutions through the courts, or obtaining local control over federal programs, are some of the ways in which Indians used electoral system mechanisms and democratic principles to get influence over Indian affairs in the 1970s. With respect to the current Indian political agenda, they are still viable strategies.

THE FOUNDATION FOR A CONTEMPORARY INDIAN POLITICAL AGENDA

Today's Indian political agenda, although the specific issues are somewhat different, contains given priorities that have changed very little from one policy-making epoch to another. What is different is the Indians' increased ability to get favorable outcomes on these issues. Consequently, Indian politics continues to be preoccupied with treaty rights, reciprocal rights and obligations associated with the trust relationship, and the question of Indian political status—issues dealing with sovereignty, self-determination, and self-governance. Although definitive answers to these questions may never be decided, Indians have made major strides in advancing their political agenda with respect to each of these priorities. For example, the preoccupation with Indian sovereignty—political autonomy and independence—is reflected in policy questions that deal with state and tribal jurisdiction, hunting and fishing rights, water rights, recognition and restoration of tribal status, land claims, settlements, boundaries, and gaming, all of which are currently major areas of contention in Indian affairs and with respect to which Indian interests are making significant gains.[1]

The Indian affairs agenda with respect to reciprocity in the trust relationship is reflected in policy issues that deal with social welfare and economic development. For example, Indian interests that seek to increase federal spending on the reservations and in urban environments are proceeding on the basis of their understanding that the federal government is legally and morally the trustee of the welfare of Indian populations. Similarly, economic development strategies and approaches are predicated upon the awareness that the federal government has as much responsibility for helping Indian communities to develop their natural resources and business interests as Indians do for becoming economically self-sufficient. These inherent, all-important, dimensions of the Indian political agenda—that Indian tribes and populations have a legal, moral, and constitutional right both to determine their own political destinies *and* to be protected by the federal government—are poorly understood outside of Indian country and the rarified environment of Indian affairs policy. It becomes evident, however, that the contemporary Indian political agenda, which emphasizes new programs and coalitions aimed at educating the public on Indian treaty rights, reflects this awareness.

This profoundly unique dimension of Indian affairs—the constitutional mandate—actually explains why the history of Indian policy has been both inverse and progressive in its development. That is, the fact that the federal government is both the trustee and also, in some sense, equal partner with the Indian tribes, constitutes an intrinsically volatile and potentially creative relationship. It is a relationship further complicated by the federal government's dual imperatives to promote the public welfare and at the same time protect the interests of minorities. Thus, the constitutional mandate's inherent duality and the tensions associated with it mean that the Indian-federal government relationship is constantly being redefined—sometimes in furtherance of the Indian interest, at other times to its detriment.

Originally, the Indian-federal relationship was that of sovereign-to-sovereign, as attested to by the treaties. It then regressed, in this sense, through policy eras where assimilation, removal, allotment, and termination ideologies were dominant, with Indians clearly the lesser powerless partner. The growth of both the self-determination through economic development and self-governance, and constitutional sovereignty ideologies since 1970 has, however, reversed the historical trend toward lesser sovereignty.

Thus, because the pattern is inverse, Indians have experienced periodic political setbacks—for example, as in judicial decisions denying them jurisdiction over non-Indians, or in cutbacks in federal spending. Nonetheless, it can be argued that Indians have emerged from each period of regression better able to defend and achieve their political goals than they were before the regressive policy era occurred. This is precisely what happened during the 1970s when Indian policy preferences became official policy after several decades of termination policy.

Even if we are convinced, however, that Indians have acquired political power through this process of inversion and progression, major questions remain. Most of these have to do with the willingness and ability of Indian populations to capitalize on the political lessons of the past. Therefore, they are questions that are not easy to answer because policy outcomes favorable to Indian interests will depend on two factors: the Indians' ability to create and maintain the resources necessary for obtaining influence over the policy agenda, and the development of attitudes that will value setting aside traditionalism and ambivalence over political status long enough to pursue policy goals and strategies that will benefit all Indians.

In short, the success of the modern Indian political agenda will depend on the ability of Indian constituencies to develop and apply the conventional mechanisms of political power and influence in continuing to act as interests groups and through the further development of political bases on reservations and in the cities. The following two imaginary scenarios illustrate this conclusion. The first scenario speculates about what might happen if Indians don't use the Constitution and electoral system principles to extend past gains and advance a new agenda. The second scenario suggests how Indians are even now, despite great odds, using democratic principles to maximize the gains of the seventies and develop their political assets.

THE INDIAN POLITICAL AGENDA: PRESENT AND FUTURE SCENARIOS

In the first scenario, Indian politics would revert to its pre-sixties outlook. Thus, except for a very few of the larger, already politically influential, resource-rich tribes, like the Navajo or northern Cheyenne, we would expect Indian tribal affairs to be dominated by the BIA and other agencies of the federal government. These communities, for example, would be reluctant or unable to take advantage of the contracting legislation, or of new economic development opportunities. Therefore, instead of operating their own programs, or engaging in joint economic ventures, Scenario Number One communities would let these activities remain with the traditional Indian agencies and leave economic development up to non-Indian companies.

Thus, the conditions of poverty and unemployment in Scenario Number One communities would remain as they are, or worsen. This would be due, in part, to the continuation of present trends in federal cutbacks for social welfare spending, and partly because these communities would have done very little to develop tribal leadership or to continue to educate young people who, as lawyers and other professionals, might return home to help Scenario Number One communities achieve their economic, social, and political ambitions. Furthermore, in Scenario Number One communities, deeply rooted historical tendencies and attitudes that tie the community's fortunes to the proven vicissitudes of government spending or to a preoccupation with the federal government's motives, with respect to termination or unilaterally ending the trust relationship, would continue to interfere with the development of strong and independent initiatives for growth.

Accordingly, very little of significance would be done to develop the community's own resources and economic potential and, thereby, to create alternatives to dependency. By the same token, the blind side of Indian politics—the inclination to want to stay out of the white world, which also means avoiding competing directly with non-Indian interests—would flourish. Consequently, Scenario Number One communities would be unable to see the value of educating the non-Indian public on the question of Indian treaty rights and the trust relationship. They will thus undermine their ability to win land-related and jurisdictional confrontations with local governments.

Finally, Scenario Number One Indian communities, urban as well as rural, would continue to be identified with internal factionalism and disharmony, unable to set new goals or to follow up on their plans. They would thus be noticed for their attachment to the idea of a romantic past that, instead of serving to advance their political agenda as it could, would become a substitute for decisive, forward-looking action. In urban, rural, and reservation communities of this type, we would therefore expect to find fragmentation and a lack of coordination in program administration and the delivery of services. We would also find conflict, contradictory or missing statements of policy or mission, few educated Indians in positions of authority, and frequent turnover among those holding leadership positions. These programs will provide places of employment, but they will not present a cogent or effective approach to solving Indian community problems.

In contrast, Scenario Number Two communities are those that will have capitalized on the political lessons of the 1970s. In these communities, we will find a well-educated, highly placed, influential, and entrepreneurially minded leadership. Tribal governments, or urban coalitions, as the case may be, will thus have adopted highly articulated policies affirming their intentions, not only to assume primary responsibility for the delivery of services, but also for economic development and for challenging local government on matters of jurisdiction.

In addition, they will have allocated resources for these purposes. These communities—like the Mississippi Choctaw, the Sault Saint Marie, or Bay Mills Indian communities of northern Michigan, or the Mashantucket Pequot Indians of Connecticut—will have invested, under strong leadership, in programs that demonstrate the success of gaming enterprises or that show how Indian communities contribute to the local economy instead of acting as a drain on it. Similarly, other communities, like the Alaska Native or Passamaquoddy, will show how settlement monies can be used to buy land and create profitable business enterprises.

A major goal of Scenario Number Two communities will be to become a third branch of government, if not in some ultimate constitutional sense, then at least as an equal partner in the system of intergovernmental relations. Thus, these communities will seek to be represented in the councils of government at city, county, and state levels and will want to become members of national conferences of mayors, governors, and local officials. In addition, they may want to become a partner in the funding relationships between the federal and local governments, thus expanding their economic base through federal grants and programs to local governments.

If these goals are an example of a new political agenda for Scenario Number Two communities, then obviously, by the time they reach this level of development, they will have decided that what they want is to transcend the traditional survival ethic of Indian communities and prosper—to take growth-oriented risks instead of maintaining the status quo. Thus, we might expect Indian communities of this type to invest their resources in economic development activities and in lobbying for their interests in state and national arenas. These activities will serve to provide employment and fight poverty. They will also help generate alternatives to the historical dependence on government spending. Most importantly, in exercising economic and political clout, these communities will see to it that the Indians' unique political status is not jeopardized by their economic successes, as was true during the termination era.

EXPANDING THE INDIAN POLITICAL BASE

In line with the experience gained during the 1970s, Scenario Number Two communities will make a major effort to develop political clout and influence. Thus, they will develop an approach that favors implementing conventional electoral system strategies—interest groups, elections, running for office—in behalf of their own policy goals. An Indian political approach that would thus reflect knowledge gained from the experience of the seventies, would have the following characteristics.

First, Indian political organizations will attempt to develop local Indian constituencies powerful enough to exert decisive influence on Indian policy outcomes at both local and national levels. This means that tribal and formal organizations will invest in voter registration strategies, evaluate candidates running for office before giving them their support, run their own candidates to assure that their views will be represented, and see to it that Indian voter turn-out at election time is significant and crucial to deciding the victor. In 1984, the Indian constituency at Ft. Hall, Idaho, deployed a strategy like this one. They succeeded in helping to elect a U.S. Congressman by a margin of seventy votes. He, in turn, has appointed an Indian as his campaign chair.

Indians are too few in number to rely on becoming influential voting constituencies. The main strategy of Scenario Number Two communities will be to develop effective interest groups, or to employ private lobbyists who will perform interest group functions in their behalf. As effective as the interest group strategy has been shown to be, however, it is enormously expensive. Implementing it will thus require resources that many tribes lack. Thus, Scenario Number Two communities will continue to lobby for increased federal spending for social programs.

Many tribes and Indian organizations also resist the interest group strategy because it seems less pure than basing the attempt to influence on the moral and legal imperatives contained in the trust relationship. These are internal discussions that will need to take place before Indian constituencies can take full advantage of the electoral system opportunities available to them. In addition, urban constituencies may want to ally with other minority populations, in which case voter registration and turn-out campaigns will be key strategies for them.

Rural and tribal communities, however, will not want to ignore developing themselves fully as political constituencies. In thus giving themselves improved access to the positions taken by local elected officials, Scenario Number Two communities will be much more likely to make democratically sound decisions because their members will be more directly involved in decision-making processes than they are now. One lesson of the seventies was to learn that the support of local delegations is crucial to the enactment of legislation favoring tribal Indian preferences. Another lesson was to learn that maximizing the input of those directly affected by policy decisions is preferable to imposing directives from the top down.

Scenario Number Two communities will also want to develop their capabilities as voting constituencies because Indian populations are fast-growing, very young, and therefore have the potential for becoming increasingly visible in state and local communities where they are already a numerical presence. If this group can be mobilized in behalf of tribal goals, it might very well exert more of an influence on local delegations than it has in the past, especially with respect to state-tribal jurisdictional issues. In addition, these communities may decide to run their own candidates for political office, or, where this is not possible, to actively support those candidates who are willing to take positions favorable to Indian interests. Scenario Number Two communities will also be interested in supporting national Indian organizations and in seeing to it that they continue to act, not merely as legislative watchdogs, but also as instigators of policy initiatives.

The lasting impact of the politics of the seventies was to enable

Scenario Number Two to become a reality. Thus, a contemporary Indian agenda will reflect goals that are universal rather than particular to specific Indian tribes. It will also reflect values that are increasingly in keeping with the tenor of the times. Therefore, a national Indian political agenda might contain the following purposes: (a) to participate in the American political system so that Indians can be represented in state and national legislatures by their own people; (b) to continue to bring lawsuits to the courts to fight for Indian treaty rights; (c) to systematically educate non-Indians about the reasons that Indians are entitled to special rights under the Constitution, and to try to change the attitudes of those who are prejudiced or discriminate against Indians; (d) to continue to deploy economic development strategies in order to become more self-sufficient and independent; (e) to permit tribal governments to make their own decisions about the development and use of natural resources; and (f) to continue encouraging and assisting Indians to pursue higher education.

Indian tribes and communities have been able to experience what it is like to take control over their own development. The ball has now been in the court of many of these communities since the early 1970s. How many more will benefit from the lessons of the seventies will depend on their willingness and on the resources available to them. Both of these conditions are required if Indian tribes and communities are to be able to use the advantages the political system provides them through the constitutional mandate, superior access, and the institutions of government. They have proved significant advantages indeed.

NOTE

1. This discussion of current issues is partly taken from the following newspaper indexes from 1980 to 1988: the *Washington Post*, the *New York Times*, the *Christian Science Monitor*, the *Los Angeles Times*, and the *Wall Street Journal*.

Appendix A
Note on Method

Respondents for this study were selected from lists compiled from congressional committee hearings on major legislation enacted during the 1970s. Initial listings were narrowed on the basis of those respondents who were available for face-to-face interviews (forty-two) in Washington, D.C., between June and August 1984, or for telephone interviews (twenty-four) during September and October of 1984 (see Table A.1).

The final list of interviewees reflected the effects of "snowballing." Thus, where several respondents independently recommended I make a special effort to talk to certain individuals perceived by them as especially prominent or expert in Indian affairs, I was sometimes able to add these names to those interviewed. All respondents were assured of anonymity and that they would not be quoted for attribution. All were persons knowledgeable about Indian policy, most had eleven to twenty years of experience at the time (see Table A.2). Most respondents also had law degrees and nearly all of them possessed remarkably strong and articulate views about the political forces affecting Indian policy development.

The interviews averaged approximately one and one-half hours in length. Interviewees were asked why they thought so much landmark Indian legislation had been passed in the seventies and allowed to answer in their own ways. I used probes only to clarify responses or to elicit comment about specific policies. Respondents were also invited to talk about the failure of Indian policy. None saw the seventies legislation as an example of the failure of Indian policy to achieve Indian policy preferences.

Table A.1
Number of Respondents by Race and Type of Interview

Type of Interview	Indian	Non-Indian
Face to face	13	29
Telephone	11	13
Total $\underline{N}$ = 66	24	42

Table A.2
Respondent Profiles: Experience, Education, Occupation

	Number of People	Percent
Years of experience with Indian policy:		
5 or less	4	6.1
6 to 10	7	10.6
11 to 15	31	47.0
16 to 20	12	18.2
20 or more	9	13.6
Total	N = 63*	
Education:		
Less than 12	1	1.5
12 (high school graduate)	2	3.0
13 to 15	3	4.5
16 (college graduate)	9	13.6
More than 16	15	22.7
Law degree	31	47.0
Total	N = 62*	
Occupation at time of involvement with Indian affairs in 1970s:		
Congressional staff	18	27.3
White House staff	4	6.1
Government agency	16	24.2

Table A.2 *(continued)*

	Number of People	Percent
Occupation at time of involvement with Indian affairs in 1970s:		
Nongovernment organization (Indian)	14	21.2
Nongovernment organization (Non-Indian)	2	3.0
Member of Congress	3	4.5
Lobbyist/Washington representative	7	10.6
Total	N = 64*	

*Respondents do not total sixty-six in all cases because demographic data were not forthcoming from some of them. Percentages have been rounded off to the nearest tenth.

Appendix B
Landmark Indian Legislation, 1970 to 1980

Year	Statute
1971	Alaska Native Claims Settlement Act (PL 92–203)
1972	Indian Education Act (Title IV of the Education Amendments of 1972, PL 92–318)
1973	Menominee Restoration Act (PL 93–197)
1974	Indian Financing Act (PL 93–262)
1975	American Indian Policy Review Commission (PL 93–580)
1975	Indian Self-Determination and Educational Assistance Act (PL 93–638)
1976	Indian Health Care Improvement Act (PL 94–437)
1977	Siletz Indian Tribe Restoration Act (PL 95–195)
1977	Surface Mining Control and Reclamation Act
1978	American Indian Religious Freedom Act (PL 95–341)
1978	Indian Child Welfare Act (PL 95–608)
1980	Maine Indians Claims Settlement Act (PL 96–420)

SOURCE: *Congressional Quarterly Almanac*, 1968–1980; *U.S. Statutes at Large*, 1968–1980.

Appendix C
Washington Representatives: Firms Listing Two or More American Indian Clients, Tribes, and/or Organizations in 1983[1]

Firm (N=11)

Fried, Frank, Harris, Shriver, and Kampelman

Client and Location(N=45)

Cheyenne River Sioux Tribe (Eagle Butte, SD)

Hualapai Tribe (Peach Springs, AZ)

Metlakatla Indian Community (Annette Islands Reserve, AK)

Miccosukee Tribe of Indians of Florida (Miami, FL)

Navajo Nation

Nez Perce Tribe (Lapwai, ID)

Oglala Sioux Tribe (Pine Ridge, SD)

Pueblo of Laguna (Laguna, NM)

Rosebud Sioux Tribe (Rosebud, SD)

Salt River Pima—Maricopa Community (Scottsdale, AZ)

Seneca Nation of Indians of New York (Irving, NY)

Karl A. Funke & Associates	Ft. Peck Tribe (Poplar, MT)
	Keweenaw Bay Chippewa Tribe (Baraga, MI)
	Navajo Health Foundation (Ganado, AZ)
	Penobscot Indian Nation (Indian Island, ME)
	Standing Rock Sioux Tribe (Ft. Yates, ND)
	Yakima Indian Nation (Toppenish, WA)
Ziontz, Pirtle, Moriset, Ernstof & Chestnut	Five Tribes Confederacy of North Central Oklahoma (Ponca City, OK)
	Kiowa—Comanche—Apache Intertribal Land Use Committee (Lawton, OK)
	Kootznoowoo, Inc. (Angoon, AK)
	Seneca-Cayuga Tribe of Oklahoma (Miami, OK)
	Ukpeaguik Inupiat Corporation
Wilkinson, Barker, Knauer, & Quinn	Arapahoe Tribe of Indians (Ft. Washakie, WY)
	Hoopa Valley Tribe (Hoopa, CA)
	Pueblo de Cochiti (Cochiti, NM)
	Three Affiliated Tribes of the Ft. Berthold Reservation (New Town, ND)
	Wichita and Affiliated Tribes (Anadarko, OK)
Gerard, Byler & Associates	Ak Chin Indian Community (Maricopa, AZ)
	Makah Tribal Council (Neah Bay, WA)
	Minnesota Chippewa Tribe (Cass Lake, MN)
	Tualip Tribes (Marysville, WA)
Terrance J. Brown Associates	Eastern Band of Cherokee Indians (Cherokee, NC)
	Red Lake Bank of Chippewa Indians (Red Lake, MN)

	Seneca Nation of Indians of New York (Irving, NY)
	United South and Eastern Tribes (Nashville, TN)
Cook, Purcell, Hansen Henderson	Aleutian-Pribilof Islands & Association (Anchorage, AK)
	Tanadgusix Corporation (St. Paul Island, AK)
Duncan, Weinberg & Miller	Sealaska Corporation (Juneau, AK)
	Tlingit and Haida Indian Tribes Central Council (Juneau, AK)
E. Thomas Colosimo	ARROW (Americans for Righting Restoration of Old Wrongs) (Washington, D.C.)
Sonosky, Chambers, Sachse & Guido	Assiniboine and Sioux Tribes (Ft. Peck Reservation, Poplar, MT)
	Standing Rock Sioux Tribe (Ft. Yates, ND)
Whittlesey & O'Brien	Cow Creek Bank of Umpqua Tribe of Indians (Canyonville, OR)
	Cowlitz Indian Tribe (Tacoma, WA)

SOURCE: Arthur C. Close, ed., *Washington Representatives* (Directory of Washington Representatives of American Associations and Industry). Washington, D.C.: Columbia Books, 1983.

NOTE

1. Additional firms were listed as having one Indian client. For example, in 1979, *Washington Representatives* listed twenty-four firms as representing forty-eight Indian clients. Only four of these firms had more than two Indian clients, unlike eleven who did in 1983. Interestingly, only five of the firms listed in 1979 also appear on the 1983 list.

Selected Bibliography

GENERAL REFERENCES

Ablon, Joan. "Relocated American Indians in the San Francisco Bay Area: Social Interaction and Indian Identity." *Human Organization* 23 (1964):296–304.

———. "American Indian Relocation: Problems of Dependency and Management in the City." *Phylon* 26 (1965):362–371.

———. "Retention of Cultural Values and Differential Urban Adaptation: Samoans and American Indians in a West Coast City." *Social Forces* 49 (1971):385–393.

Abourezk, Senator James. *Wassaja*/The Indian Historian. Interview, October-November 1974.

"Alaska Native Claims Settlement Act." Juneau, Alaska: *Native News* 10 (November-December 1973).

American Academy of Child Psychiatry. *Supportive Care, Custody, Placement and Adoption of American Indian Children.* National Conference Sponsored by the American Academy of Child Psychiatry, Bottle Hollow, Utah, 19–22 April 1977.

———. *Warm Springs: A Case Study Approach To Recognizing the Strengths of American Indian and Alaska Native Families.* Washington, D.C., 1980.

"Americans for Indian Opportunity." *Civil Rights Digest*, 4, 2 (Spring 1971):14–17.

Americans for Indian Opportunity: Self-Determination for Native Americans. Annual Report 1981. Washington, D.C.: Americans for Indian Opportunity, 1981.

Anchorage Community College. *Lessons On the Alaska Native Claims Settlement Act.* Book 1: *General Information.* Anchorage, Alaska: Adult Literary Laboratory, 1972.

———. *Lessons in the Alaska Native Claims Settlement Act.* Book 2: *Land.* Anchorage, Alaska: Adult Literary Laboratory, 1972.

Annin, J., and Burt, J. D. "Overview of the Indian Child Welfare Act." Unpublished paper, n.d.

Attneave, Carolyn L. "Therapy in Tribal Settings and Urban Network Intervention." *Family Process*, pp. 192–210.

Ayres, Mary Ellen. "Federal Indian Policy and Labor Statistics—A Review Essay." *Monthly Labor Review* 101 (April 1978):22–27.

"Backlash in Congress Seen As Indian Push Claims." *Congressional Quarterly* 2 (December 1978):3385–3388.

Barsh, R. L., and Henderson, J. Y. *The Road: Indian Tribes and Political Liberty.* Berkeley, Calif.: University of California Press, 1980.

Bates, Tom. "The Government's Secret War Against the Indian." *Oregon Times*, February-March 1976, pp. 14–19.

Baxter, Tom. "The Discontinuation of the Indian Student Placement Program." Unpublished paper, March 1986.

Beer, Samuel H. "In Search of a New Public Philosophy." Edited by Anthony King. *The New American Political System.* Washington, D.C.: American Enterprise Institute for Public Policy Research, 1978.

Benham, William J., Jr. "The Role of Congress in Indian Affairs." ERIC Clearinghouse Document, ED178241, December 1977.

Berkhofer, Robert F., Jr. *The Political Context of a New Indian History.* Edited by Norris Hundley. *The American Indian.* Santa Barbara, Calif.: Clio Press, Inc., 1977.

———. *The White Man's Indian: Images of the American Indian from Columbus To the President.* New York: Vintage, 1978–1979.

Berry, Jeffrey M. *Lobbying for the People.* Princeton, N.J.: Princeton University Press, 1977.

———. *The Interest Group Society.* Boston: Little, Brown and Company, 1984.

Berry, Mary Clay. *The Alaska Pipeline: The Politics of Oil and Native Land Claims.* Bloomington, Ind.: Indiana University Press, 1975.

Blanchard, Evelyn Lance, and Barsh, Russell Lawrence. "What Is Best for Tribal Children? A Response to Fischler." *Social Work* (September 1980):350–357.

Blumenthal, Walter H. *American Indians Dispossessed: Fraud in Land Cessions Forced Upon the Tribes.* Philadelphia: G. S. MacManus Company, 1955.

Bounpane, Peter A. "The Census Bureau Looks to 1990." *American Demographics* (October 1983):1–8.

Brightman, Lehman. "Dealing with Indian Issues in 1988." A talk at the
    University of Utah, Indian Awareness Week, 6 May 1988.
Brophy, William A., and Aberle, Sophie D., comps. *The Indian: America's
    Unfinished Business*. Report of the Commission on the Rights, Liberties,
    and Responsibilities of the American Indian. Norman, Okla.: University
    of Oklahoma Press, 1977.
Brown, Eddie F., and Shaughnessey, T., eds. *Education for Social Work Practice
    with American Indian Families*. Tempe, Ariz.: School of Social Work,
    Arizona State University, 1979.
Bryant, Ted. "The President's Commission on Reservation Economies." A talk
    at the University of Utah, Indian Awareness Week, 9 May 1985.
"Bureau of Indian Affairs: America's Colonial Heritage." *Look Magazine*, 2
    June 1970.
Burnette, Robert. *The Tortured Americans*. Englewood Cliffs, N.J.: Prentice-
    Hall, 1971.
Butler, Raymond V. "The Bureau of Indian Affairs: Activities Since 1945."
    Annals (AAPSS) 436 (March 1978):50–60.
Button, James W. *Black Violence: Political Impact of the 1960s Riots*. N.J.:
    Princeton University Press, 1978.
Byler, W., ed. *The Destruction of the American Indian Family*. New York:
    Association of American Indian Affairs, 1977.
Cahn, Edgar S. *Our Brother's Keeper: The Indian in White America*. New York:
    World Publishing Company, 1969, 1970.
"Cameras Over Here! And Be Sure to Shoot My Good Side." *TV Guide*, 15
    December 1973, pp. 43–49.
Chapman, William. "Native Americans' New Clout." *The Progressive*, August
    1977, pp. 30–32.
Chino, Wendell, and Townsend, Miller. National Tribal Chairmen's Associa-
    tion, Letter of 20 April 1977 in AIPRC, *Final Report*, 2, pp. 570–572.
Chippewa Treaty Rights: Hunting . . . Fishing . . . Gathering on Ceded Territory.
    Odanah, Wis.: The Great Lakes Indian Fish and Wildlife Commission,
    n.d.
*[A] Chronological List of Treaties and Agreements Made by Indian Tribes with
    the United States*. Washington, D.C.: Institute for the Development of
    Indian Law, 1973.
Cingolani, William. "Acculturating the Indian: Federal Policies, 1832–1973."
    Social Work (November 1973):24–28.
Civil Rights Digest. Summer 1969, pp. 6–13.
Coffer, William E. (Hoi Hosh). *Phoenix: The Decline and Rebirth of the Indian
    People*. New York: Van Nostrand Reinhold Company, 1979.
Cohen, Felix, S. *Handbook of Federal Indian Law*, with reference to tables and
    index. Washington, D.C.: Government Printing Office, 1942. Abridged,
    1945. Reprint. Charlottesville, Va.: Michie Bobbs-Merrill, 1982.
"Committees Back Improved Health Care for Indians." *Congressional Quar-
    terly*, 22 May 1976, pp. 1281–1282.
Congressional Quarterly Almanac. 1968 through 1980 (1978, pp. 574–575; 25
    December 1971; 27 January 1973; 22 May 1976, pp. 1281–1282; 2 De-
    cember 1978; 14 June 1980, pp. 1649–1651).

Congressional Quarterly Weekly. 1968 through 1980.

Cook, James. "New Hope in the Reservations." *Forbes Magazine,* 9 November 1981, pp. 108–115.

Cornell, George. "Contemporary American Indian Issues." A talk at the University of Utah, Indian Awareness Week, 4 May 1988.

Cornell, Stephen. "The New Indian Politics." *Wilson Quarterly,* New Year's 1986, pp. 113–131.

Corrigan, Richard. "Resources Report Settlement of Native Land Claims Could Affect Alaska Pipeline Controversy." *National Journal,* 7 April 1971, pp. 837–843.

Costo, Rupert. "The American Indian and Environmental Issues." *Wassaja/ The Indian Historian* 13,2 (April 1979):51–55.

Costo, Rupert, and Henry, Jeannette. *Indian Treaties: Two Centuries of Dishonor.* San Francisco: Indian Historian Press, 1977.

Daviss, Ben. "To Stand Alone." *Continental Magazine,* November 1984, pp. 36–38, 77–81.

Dellwo, Robert D. Letter, AIPRC, *Final Report* 2 (4 May 1977):301.

Deloria, Vine, Jr. *Custer Died for Your Sins: An Indian Manifesto.* London: MacMillan, 1969.

———. *We Talk, You Listen: New Tribes, New Turf.* New York: Delta, 1970.

———. comp. *Of Utmost Good Faith.* San Francisco: Straight Arrow Books, 1971.

———. *God Is Red.* New York: Grosset and Dunlap, 1973.

———. *Behind the Trail of Broken Treaties: An Indian Declaration of Independence.* New York: Delta, 1974.

Deloria, Vine, Jr., and Lytle, Clifford M. *American Indians, American Justice.* Austin, Tex.: University of Texas Press, 1983.

———. *The Nations Within: The Past and Future of American Indian Sovereignty.* New York: Pantheon Books, 1984.

Dexter, Lewis A. *Elite and Specialized Interviewing.* Evanston, Ill.: Northwestern University Press, 1970.

Directions. "People of the Dawn." ABC Television Network. Transcript, 15 February 1981.

Dye, Thomas R. *Understanding Public Policy,* 4th ed. Englewood Cliffs, N.J.: Prentice-Hall, 1981.

Echohawk, Larry. "Indian Legal Issues." A talk at the University of Utah, Indian Awareness Week, 2 May 1988.

Edmunds, David. "Two Case Histories." *The Wilson Quarterly,* New Year's 1986, pp. 132–142.

"[The] Effects of OEO and Other Local 'Participatory Programs': Oklahomans for Indian Opportunity." Edited by Jack Rothman. *Promoting Social Justice in the Multigroup Society: A Casebook for Group Relations Practitioners.* New York: Association Press, 1971.

Eggan, Fred. *The American Indian: Perspectives for the Study of Social Change.* Cambridge: Cambridge University Press, 1966.

Embry, Carlos B. *America's Concentration Camps: The Facts About Our Indian Reservations Today.* New York: D. McKay Company, 1956.

Evarts, Jeremiah. *Essays On the Present Crisis in the Condition of the American Indian*. Boston: Perkins and Marvin, 1829.

Fellin, Phillip. "Research Teaching With Minority Content." Unpublished paper, July 1980.

Fenno, Richard F. *Congressmen in Committees*. Boston: Little, Brown and Company, 1973.

Fischler, Ronald S. "Protecting American Indian Children." *Social Work*, September 1980, pp. 341–349.

Flood, Laurence B. "Ethnic Politics and Political Science: A Survey of Leading Journals." *Ethnicity* 7 (1980):96–101.

Forbes, John. "The Anishinable Liberation Movement." *Harvard Civil Rights-Civil Liberties Law Review* 8 (1973).

Forman, Grant. *Indian Removal: The Emigration of the Five Civilized Tribes of Indians*. Norman, Okla.: University of Oklahoma Press, 1932.

Freeman, J. Leiper. *The Political Process: Executive Bureau-Legislative Committee Relations*. New York: Random House, 1955. Reprint. 1964.

Friends Committee on National Legislation (*The Indian Report[s]*) for: I-17 February 1983; I-19, March 1984, pp. 1, 5; I-27, Late Spring 1987; I-20, Summer 1984, p. 4; No. 496, November 1986; I-24, Summer 1985; I-29, Spring 1988; No. 505, August/September 1987.

Garvin, Charles. "Ethnic Analysis and Social Work Intervention." Paper prepared for presentation at the 22nd APM, Council on Social Work Education, Philadelphia, 3 March 1976.

Gessner, Robert. *Massacre: A Survey of Today's American Indian*. New York: J. Cape & H. Smith, 1931.

Gillenkirk, Jeff, and Dowie, Mark. "The Great Indian Power Grab." *Mother Jones*, January 1982, pp. 18–27, 46–52.

Goodluck, Charlotte, and Brown, Mary Ellen. "Decision Making Regarding American Indian Children and Foster Care." Phoenix, Ariz.: Jewish Family and Children's Service of Phoenix, n.d.

Grandbois, G. H. "Bureaucratization in Indian Organizations." *Journal of Humanics* 10(1) (1983):44–55.

Hagan, William T. *American Indians*. Chicago: University of Chicago Press, 1971.

———. *The Indian Rights Association: The Herbert Welsh Years 1882–1904*. Tucson, Ariz.: The University of Arizona Press, 1985.

Hall, Gilbert L. *The Federal Indian Relationship*. Washington, D.C.: Institute for the Development of Indian Law, 1979.

Harris, Fred, and Harris, LaDonna. "Indians, Coal, and the Big Sky." *The Progressive*, 1974, pp. 1–5.

Hayes, Michael T. "The Semisovereign Pressure Groups: A Critique of Current Theory and An Alternative Typology." *Journal of Politics* 4 (1978):134–161.

Heclo, Hugh. "Issue Networks and the Executive Establishment." Edited by Anthony King. *The New American Political System*. Washington, D.C.: American Enterprise Institute, 1978.

Henry, Jeannette, and Costo, Rupert. "Who Is An Indian?" *Wassaja*/The Indian Historical 13 (June 1980):15–18.

Hertzberg, Hazel W. *The Search for An American Indian Identity: Modern Pan-Indian Movements.* Syracuse, N.Y.: Syracuse University Press, 1971.

Hickel, Walter J. "Response to Strickland and Gregory." *Commonweal* 93 (16 October 1970).

———. *Who Owns America?* New York: Prentice-Hall, 1971.

Hickey, Neil. "Only the Sensational Stuff Got On the Air." *TV Guide,* 8 December 1973, pp. 34–40.

Holsti, Ole R. *Content Analysis for the Social Sciences and Humanities.* Reading Mass.: Addison-Wesley Publishing Company, 1969.

Horsman, Reginald. "American Indian Policy in the Old Northwest, 1783–1812." Edited by Rogers L. Nichols. *The American Indian: Past and Present,* 2nd ed. New York: John Wiley and Sons, 1971, 1981.

———. *Race and Manifest Destiny: The Origins of American Racial Anglo-Saxonism.* Cambridge, Mass.: Harvard University Press, 1981.

"How To Exploit and Destroy A People: The Case of the Alaska Native." *Civil Rights Digest* 2 (Summer 1969):6–13.

Hundley, Norris, Jr., ed. *The American Indian.* Santa Barbara, Calif.: American Bibliographical Center—Clio Press, Inc., 1974.

"Indian Health: Better Than It Was But Not Good Enough." *Congressional Quarterly,* 14 June 1980, pp. 1649–1651.

Indian Rights Association. *Vicious Indian Legislation, A Brief Analysis of Bills Now Pending in Congress That Ought To Be Defeated.* Philadelphia, 1916.

"Indians Hit the Road Over Backlash in Washington." *National Journal,* 26 August 1978, pp. 1353–1355.

Jackson, Curtis, E., and Galli, Marcia J. *A History of the Bureau of Indian Affairs and Its Activities Among Indians.* San Francisco: R & E Associates, 1977.

Jackson, Helen M. *A Century of Dishonor: A Sketch of the United States Government's Dealings With Some of the Indian Tribes.* Minneapolis: Ross & Haines, 1964.

Johansen, Bruce, and Maestas, Robert. *Wa si'chu: The Continuing Indian Wars.* New York: Monthly Review Press, 1979.

Jones, Dorothy V. *License for Empire: Colonialism By Treaty in Early America.* Chicago: University of Chicago Press, 1982.

Jones, Richard S. *Federal Programs of Assistance To American Indians.* Washington, D.C.: U.S. Government Printing Office, 1982.

Jorgensen, Joseph G. *The Sun Dance Relation: Power for the Powerless.* Chicago: University of Chicago Press, 1972.

Josephy, Alvin M., Jr. *Red Power: The American Indians' Fight for Freedom.* New York: McGraw-Hill, 1971, 1972.

———. *Now That the Buffalo's Gone: A Study of Today's American Indians.* Norman, Okla.: University of Oklahoma Press, 1984.

Journal of Social Issues, Research Among Racial, and Cultural Minorities: Problems, Prospects, and Pitfalls 33(4) (1977).

Kellogg, Mark. "Indian Rights: Fighting Back With White Man's Weapons." *Saturday Review* 25 (November 1978):24–30.

Kennedy, Senator Edward. "Let the Indians Run Indian Policy." *Look Magazine*, 2 June 1970, pp. 36, 38.

Kessel, JoAnn, and Robbins, Susan P. "The Indian Child Welfare Act: Dilemmas and Needs." *Child Welfare*, May-June 1984, pp. 225–232.

Kickingbird, Kirke, and Ducheneaux, Karen. *One Hundred Million Acres*. New York: MacMillan, 1973.

Kickingbird, Kirke, Skibine, Alexander Tallchief, and Kickingbird, Lynn. *Indian Jurisdiction*. Washington, D.C.: Institute for the Development of Indian Law, 1983.

Kingdon, John W. *Agendas, Alternatives and Public Policies*. Boston: Little, Brown and Company, 1984.

Kinney, Jay P. *A Continent Lost—A Civilization Won: Indian Land Tenure in America*. Baltimore: Johns Hopkins University Press, 1937.

Klausner, Samuel Z., & Foulks, Edward F. *Eskimo Capitalists: Oil, Politics, and Alcohol*. Totowa, N.J.: Allanheld, Osmun Publishers, 1982.

Knight, Michael. "Gains Affirm Indians' Rights Demands." *New York Times*, 9 July 1979, p. 10.

Krippendorff, Klaus. *Content Analysis: An Introduction To Its Methodology*. Beverly Hills, Calif.: Sage, 1980.

LaCourse, Richard. "Indian Politics in Changing Times." *Race Relations Reporter* 4 (25 June 1973).

Langford, Lord. *Nixon: A Study in Extremes of Fortune*. London: Widenfeld and Nicolson, 1980.

Lazarus, Arthur, Jr. "The Alaska Native Claims Settlement Act: A Flawed Victory." *Law and Contemporary Problems* 40 (Winter 1976):132–165.

League of Women Voters. "The Menominee: A Case Against Termination." *The Voter*, January-February 1973, pp. 17–20.

Leupp, Francis E. *The Indian and His Problem*. New York: Charles Scribner's Sons, 1910.

LeVeen, Deborah. "Organization or Disruption? Strategic Options for Marginal Groups: The Case of the Chicago Indian Village." Edited by Jo Freeman. *Social Movements of the Sixties and Seventies*. New York: Longman, 1983.

Levitan, Sar A., and Johnston, William B. *Indian Giving: Federal Programs for Native Americans*. Baltimore, Md.: Johns Hopkins University Press, 1975.

Lichtenstein, Grace. "Indian Tribes Are Using the System To Win Rights." *New York Times*, 21 December 1975, p. 31.

Light, Larry. "Land at Stake: Backlash in Congress Seen As Indians Push Claims." *Congressional Quarterly*, 2 December 1978, pp. 3385–3388.

Linscheid, Steve. *Federal Trust Responsibility and Indian Tribes* (Background Papers On Native American Issues). Washington, D.C.: Friends Committee on National Legislation, September 1982.

———. *Indian Water Rights* (Background Papers On Native American Issues). Washington, D.C.: Friends Committee On National Legislation, September 1982.

Loomis, Burdett A., and Cigler, Allan J. "The Changing Nature of Interest Group Politics." Edited by Alan J. Cigler and Burdett A. Loomis. *Interest Group Politics*. Washington, D.C.: Congressional Quarterly Press, 1983.

Lowi, Theodore. "American Business, Public Policy, Case Studies and Political Theory." *World Politics* 16 (July 1964):677–715.

––––––. "Distribution, Regulation, Redistribution: The Functions of Government." Edited by Randall B. Ripley. *Public Policies and Their Publics.* New York: Norton, 1966.

Lurie, Nancy. "Menominee Termination: From Reservation To Colony." *Human Organization* 31(3) (Fall 1972):257–270.

––––––. "The World's Oldest On-Going Protest Demonstration: North American Indian Drinking Patterns." Edited by Norris Hundley. *The American Indian.* Santa Barbara, Calif.: American Bibliographical Center—Clio Press, 1974.

McBeath, Gerald A., and Morehouse, Thomas A. *The Dynamics of Alaska Native Self-Government.* Lanham, Md.: University Press of America, 1981.

McCreight, Major Israel. *Firewater and Forked Tongues: A Sioux Chief Interprets U.S. History.* Pasadena, Calif.: Trails End Publishing Company, 1947.

McLaughlin, Robert. "Giving It Back To the Indians." *Atlantic,* February 1977, pp. 70–85.

McNickle, D'Arcy. *They Came Here First: The Epic of the American Indian.* New York: J. B. Lippincott, 1949.

Marousek, L. A. "The ICWA of 1978: Provisions and Policy." *South Dakota Law Review* 25 (Winter 1980):98–115.

Medcalf, Linda. *Law and Identity: Lawyers, Native Americans, and Legal Practice.* Beverly Hills, Calif.: Sage Publications, 1978.

Meriam, Lewis. *The Problem of Indian Administration.* Baltimore, Md.: Johns Hopkins University Press, 1928.

Merrick, Janna C. "Treaty Indian Fishing Rights: Developments in Washington State." Paper delivered at the 1979 Annual Meeting of the APSA, Washington, D.C., 30 August–3 September 1979.

Michener, James A. *Centennial.* N.Y.: Random House, 1974.

Miller, D. L.; Hoffman, F.; and Turner, D. "A Perspective On the ICWA." *Social Casework* 61 (1980):468–471.

Mindell, Carl E., M.D., and Gurwitt, Alan, M.D. *The Placement of American Indian Children—The Need for Change.* Washington, D.C.: American Academy of Child Psychiatry, January 1975.

Morris, Aldon D. *The Origins of the Civil Rights Movement: Black Communities Organizing for Change.* New York: The Free Press, 1984.

Nagata, Suichi. "The Reservation Community and the Urban Community: Hopi Indians of Noenkopi." Edited by Jack O. Waddell and Michael O. Watson. *The American Indian in Urban Society.* Boston: Little, Brown and Company, 1971.

Nammack, Georgianna C. *Fraud, Politics, and the Dispossession of the Indians: The Iroquois Land Frontier and the Colonial Period.* Norman, Okla.: University of Oklahoma Press, 1969.

National Council on Indian Opportunity. *Report.* Washington, D.C., 28 April 1970. (Typewritten.)

––––––. "Project Outreach Report: An Assessment of Tribal Attitudes and Appraisal of the Extent of Tribal Council Experience in Administering Federal Assistance Programs." Washington, D.C., n.d. (Typewritten.)

[The]National Journal, 1968 through 1970 (26 August 1978).

"[The] Native Americans." *Youth* 24 (November 1973).

New York Times. 1969 through 1972.

Nichols, Roger L. *The American Indian: Past and Present*, 2nd ed. New York: John Wiley and Sons, 1981.

Nixon, Richard. *The Memoirs of Richard Nixon.* New York: Grosset & Dunlap, 1978.

Officer, James E. *The American Indian and Federal Policy.* Edited by Jack O. Waddell and O. Michael Watson. *The American Indian in Urban Society.* Boston: Little, Brown and Company, 1971.

"One Indian's Fight Against Termination." *San Francisco Chronicle*, 5 May 1973, p. 14.

Orfield, Gary. *A Study of the Termination Policy.* Completed for the National Congress of American Indians, 1965.

————. "Menominee Restoration." *Civil Rights Digest* 6 (Fall 1973):34–40.

Oswalt, Wendell H. *This Land Was Theirs: A Study of the North American Indian.* New York: John Wiley and Sons, 1966.

"Our Media Blitz Is Here to Stay." *TV Guide*, 22 December 1973, pp. 221–223.

"[A] Paleface Uprising." *Newsweek*, 10 April 1978, pp. 39–40.

Peithmann, Irvin M. *Broken Peace Pipes: A Four Hundred Year History of the American Indian.* Springfield, Ill.: Thomas, 1964.

Peroff, Nicholas C. *Menominee Drums: Tribal Termination and Restoration, 1954–1974.* Norman, Okla.: University of Oklahoma Press, 1982.

Pevar, Stephen L. *The Rights of Indians and Tribes.* New York: Bantam Books, 1983.

Piven, Frances Fox. *Poor Peoples' Movements: Why They Succeed, How They Fail.* N.Y.: Pantheon, 1977.

Piven, Frances Fox, and Cloward, Richard A. *Regulating the Poor: The Functions of Public Welfare.* N.Y.: Vintage, Random House, 1971.

Price, David E. "Policy Making in Congressional Committees: The Impact of 'Environmental' Factors." *APSR* 72 (1978):548–574.

Price, John A. "The Migration and Adaptation of American Indians to Los Angeles." *Human Organization* 27 (1968):168–175.

Priest, Loring Benson. *Uncle Sam's Stepchildren: The Reformation of U.S. Indian Policy, 1865–1887.* New Brunswick, N.J.: Rutgers University Press, 1942.

Prucha, Francis Paul. "Andrew Jackson's Indian Policy: A Reassessment." *Journal of American History* 56 (December 1969):527–539.

————. *American Indian Policy in the Formative Years: The Indian Trade and Intercourse Acts 1790–1834.* Lincoln, Nebr.: University of Nebraska Press, 1962, 1970.

————. ed. *Americanizing the American Indians: Writings by the "Friends of the Indian" 1880–1900.* Lincoln, Nebr.: University of Nebraska Press, 1973.

————. *A Bibliographic Guide To the History of Indian-White Relations in the United States.* Chicago: University of Chicago Press, 1977.

————. *Indian-White Relations in the United States: A Bibliography of Works Published 1975–1980*. Lincoln, Nebr.: University of Nebraska Press, 1982.

Rader, Brian F. *The Political Outsiders: Blacks and Indians in a Rural Oklahoma County*. San Francisco: R & E Research Associates, 1978.

Raymer, Patricia, and Raymer, Steve. "Wisconsin's Menominees: Indians On a Seesaw." *National Geographic* 146(2) (August 1974):228–251.

"Red Man's Revenge." *Saturday Review*, 30 September 1978, p. 10.

"Remarks on 'Humoring' Indians Bring Protest From Tribal Leaders." *New York Times*, 1 June 1988, p. 7, A13.

"Report On the Urban Indian in Portland." *Portland City Club Bulletin* 56 (27 October 1975):22.

Ridley, J. R. "Indian Organizations: A General Overall View." *American Indian Culture Center Journal* 4 (1973):15–18.

Ritt, Leonard G. "Some Social and Political Views of American Indians." *Ethnicity* 6 (1979):45–72.

Rohrer, S. Scott. "Indians Hit the Road Over Backlash in Washington." *National Journal*, 26 August 1978, pp. 1353–1355.

"Ruling Favoring Utes Leaves Duchesne Nervous." *The Salt Lake Tribune*, 7 December 1986, pp. B–1, B–3.

Schultz, Terri. "Bamboozle Me Not At Wounded Knee." *Harper's*, June 1973, pp. 46–56.

Scott, Wilfred. "Energy Resource Tribes Have More To Offer the Nation Than the Usual Hot Air." *Wassaja/The Indian Historical* 13(3) (September 1980):13–16.

Sheehan, Bernard W. *Seeds of Extinction: Jeffersonian Philanthropy and the American Indian*. Chapel Hill, N.C.: University of North Carolina Press, 1973.

Smith, Desmond. "The Media Coup D'Etat." *The Nation*, 25 June 1973.

Sorkin, Alan L. *The Urban American Indian*. Lexington, Mass.: Lexington Books, 1978.

Speck, Ross V., and Attneave, Carolyn L. *Family Networks*. New York: Pantheon Books, 1973.

Spicer, Edward H. *The American Indians*. Cambridge, Mass.: Harvard University Press, 1982.

Spindler, George D., and Spindler, Louise S. "Identity, Militancy, and Cultural Congruence: The Menominee and Kainai." *The Annals* 436 (March 1978):73–85.

[The] Status of the Termination of the Menominee Indian Tribe (Report to Congress Describing the Effects After Four Years of Termination). Washington, D.C.: The Bureau of Indian Affairs, February 1965.

Steiner, Stan. *The New Indians*. New York: Dell Publishing Company, 1968.

Strickland, Rennard. "An Open Letter to President Reagan On Indian Law and Policy." Kennedy School of Government, Public Forum, Harvard University, 12 November 1980.

Strickland, Rennard, and Gregory, Jack. "Nixon and the Indians: Is Dick Another Buffalo Bill?" *Commonweal* 92 (4 September 1970:432–436.

Svensson, Frances. *The Ethnics in American Politics: American Indians*. Minneapolis, Minnesota: Burgess Publishing Company, 1973.

———. "Language As Ideology: The American Indian Case." *American Indian Culture and Research Journal* 1 (1975):29–35.

Taylor, Theodore W. *American Indian Policy*. Mt. Airy, Md.: Lomond Publications, 1983.

Thomas, Robert K. "Pan-Indianism." Edited by D. E. Walker. *The Emergent Native Americans*. Boston: Little, Brown and Company, 1977.

Trimble, Joseph E. "The Sojourner in the American Indian Community: Methodological Issues and Concerns." *Journal of Social Issues* (1977):159–162.

Trosper, Ronald L. "Native American Boundary Maintenance: The Flathead Indian Reservation, Montana, 1860–1970." *Ethnicity* 3 (1976):256–276.

Tyler, Lyman S. *A Study of the Changes in Policy of the United States Toward Indians*. Salt Lake City, Utah: University of Utah Libraries, n.d.

———. *A History of Indian Policy*. Washington, D.C.: U.S. Government Printing Office, 1973.

Uncommon Controversy: Fishing Rights of the Muckelshoot, Puyallup, and Nisqually Indians (A Report Prepared for the American Friends Service Committee). Seattle: University of Washington Press, 1970.

Unger, Steven, ed. *The Destruction of American Indian Families*. New York: Association of American Indian Affairs, 1978.

United Effort Trust (in cooperation with the Institute for the Development of Indian Law and the American Indian Law Center). "Indian Claims and Indian Water Rights." Washington, D.C., n.d.

———. "Land Claims." Washington, D.C., n.d.

U.S. Commission on Civil Rights. "Staff Memorandum: Constitutional Status of American Indians." March 1973.

Van Every, Dale. *Disinherited: The Lost Birthright of the American Indian*. New York: Morrow, 1966.

Veeder, William. "Indian Water Rights and the National Water Commission." *Civil Rights Digest* 6(1) (Fall 1973):28–33.

Viola, Herman J. "Indians Braved Washington To See the 'Great Father'." *Smithsonian* 12(1) (April 1981):72–80.

Vogel, Virgil J. *This Country Was Ours: A Documentary History of the American Indian*. New York: Harper Torchbooks, 1972.

Waddell, Jack O., and Watson, Michael O., eds. *The American Indian in Urban Society*. Boston: Little, Brown and Company, 1971.

Waldron, Martin. "U.S. Indians Press Drive To Get Independent Status." *New York Times*, 19 August 1974, pp. 1, 36.

Walker, Jack L. "Setting the Agenda in the U.S. Senate: A Theory of Problem Selection." *British Journal of Political Science* 7 (October 1977):423–445.

———. "The Origins and Maintenance of Interest Groups in America." *APSR* 77(2) (June 1983):390–406.

Washburn, Wilcomb E. "Legitimate Indian Leaders." Letter to the Editor. *Wilson Quarterly*, Autumn 1986.

————. *Red Man's Land—White Man's Law*. New York: Charles Scribner's Sons, 1971.

————. "The Writing of American Indian History: A Status Report." Edited by Norris Hundley. *The American Indian: Essays From the Pacific Historical Review*. Santa Barbara, Calif.: Clio Press, Inc., 1974.

————. *The Indian in America*. New York: Harper & Row, 1975.

Wassaja. October-November, 1974, p. 13; September-October 1982.

Watkins, Arthur V. "Termination of Federal Supervision: The Removal of Restrictions Over Indian Property and Person." *The Annals* CCCXI (May 1957):47–55.

Wax, Murray L. *Indian Americans: Unity and Diversity*. Englewood Cliffs, N.J.: Prentice-Hall, 1971.

[The]White House, Office of the Press Secretary. Press Release of 14 January 1983.

Whiteman, Henrietta. "Changes in Indian Women's Roles." A talk at the University of Utah, Indian Awareness Week, 5 May 1988.

Wilder, Leroy W. "Rights and Responsibilities of Indian Tribes and State Agencies Under the Indian Child Welfare Act." Unpublished paper, n.d.

Wilson, Ernest J. III. "Why Political Scientists Don't Study Black Politics, But Historians and Sociologists Do." *PS* (Summer 1985):600–607.

Wilson, James Q. *Political Organizations*. New York: Basic Books, 1973.

"Wisconsin's Menominees: Indians On a Seesaw." *National Geographic*, August 1974, pp. 228–251.

Woll, Peter. *Public Policy*. Cambridge, Mass.: Winthrop Publishers, Inc., 1974.

Yinger, Milton J., and Simpson, George E. "The Integration of Americans of Indian Descent." *The Annals (AAPSS)* 436 (March 1978):131–151.

Youth: The Native Americans. Philadelphia: United Church Press, November 1973.

Youth Policy and Law Center, Inc. "Indian Child Welfare Act." Madison, Wisconsin, n.d.

GOVERNMENT DOCUMENTS AND PUBLICATIONS

House Committees

U.S. Congress. House. Committee on Interior and Insular Affairs. *Hearings On the Menominee Restoration Act*. Hearings before the Subcommittee on Indian Affairs, 93rd Congress, 1st Session, 25–26 May 1973; 28 June 1973.

————. *Alaska Native Land Claims Part II* (Serial 91–8). Hearings before the Subcommittee on Indian Affairs, 17–18 October 1969.

————. *Alaska Native Land Claims*. Hearings before the Subcommittee on Indian Affairs, 92nd Congress, 1st Session, 3–7 May 1971.

————. *Hearings On the Indian Health Care Improvement Act*. Hearings before the Subcommittee on Indian Affairs, 93rd Congress, 2nd Session, 25–26 September 1975.

U.S. Congress. House. Committee on Interstate and Foreign Commerce. *State-*

ment of the American College of Obstetricians and Gynecologists on the Indian Health Care Improvement Act. Hearings before the Subcommittee on Public Health and Environment by Ervin E. Nichols, M.D., 28 April 1976.

House Reports and Miscellaneous Documents

U.S. Congress. House. *Providing for the Settlement of Land Claims of Alaska Natives.* 92nd Congress, 1st Session, 28 September 1971. (Mimeographed.)

———. *Alaska Native Claims Settlement Act.* Conference Report 92–746 to accompany HR 10367, 92nd Congress, 1st Session, 13 December 1971.

———. *Repealing the Act Terminating Federal Supervision Over the Property and the Members of the Menominee Indian Tribe of Wisconsin.* H. Report 93–572, 93rd Congress, 1st Session, 11 October 1973.

———. *Establishing Standards for the Placement of Indian Children in Foster or Adoptive Homes, To Prevent the Breakup of Indian Families, and for Other Purposes.* H. Report 1386, 95th Congress, 2nd Session, 24 July 1978.

U.S. Congress Senate: American Indian Policy Review Commission

Report On Indian Education. Task Force Five. Washington, D.C.: U.S. Government Printing Office, 1976.

Report On Indian Health. Task Force Six. Washington, D.C.: U.S. Government Printing Office, 1976.

Report On Alcohol and Drug Abuse. Task Force Eleven. Washington, D.C.: U.S. Government Printing Office, 1976.

Final Report To the Congress, 17 May 1977. Vol. 1. Washington, D.C.: U.S. Government Printing Office, 1977.

Final Report: Appendices and Index. Vol. 2. Washington, D.C.: U.S. Government Printing Office, 1977.

Special Joint Task Force Report on Alaskan Native Issues. Washington, D.C.: U.S. Government Printing Office, 1976

Senate Committees

U.S. Congress. Senate. Committee on Labor and Public Welfare, Special Committee on Indian Education. *Indian Education: A National Tragedy—A National Challenge.* S. Report 91–501, 91st Congress, 1st Session, 1969.

———. Committee on Interior and Insular Affairs. *Hearings On the Alaska Native Claims Settlement Act of 1970,* 91st Congress, 2nd Session, 11 June 1970.

———. *Hearings On Alaska Native Land Claims,* 92nd Congress, 1st Session, 18 February 1971, 16 March 1971.

———. *Hearings On the Indian Health Care Improvement Act.* Hearings before the Subcommittee on Indian Affairs, 93rd Congress, 2nd Session, 3, 5 April 1974.

———. *Problems That American Indian Families Face in Raising Their Children and How These Problems Are Affected by Federal Action or Inaction.* Hearings before the Subcommittee on Indian Affairs, 93rd Congress, 2nd Session, 8–9 April 1974.

U.S. Congress. Senate. Senate Select Committee on Indian Affairs. *Hearings On Senate 1214, The Indian Child Welfare Act,* 95th Congress, 2nd Session, 4 August 1977.

Senate Reports and Miscellaneous Documents

U.S. Department of Interior, Task Force on Indian Affairs. *Report to the Secretary of the Interior.* 10 July 1961. (Mimeographed.)

———. Bureau of Indian Affairs. *The Status of the Termination of the Menominee Indian Tribe* (by Gary Orfield). Report to the Congress Describing the Effects After Four Years of Termination. February 1965.

U.S. President. President Johnson's Message to Congress on "The Forgotten American." *Congressional Quarterly Almanac,* 6 March 1968, pp. 77A–80A.

———. President Nixon's Message to Congress on "Indian Self-Determination." *Congressional Quarterly Almanac,* 8 July 1970, pp. 101A–105A.

———. *Alaska Native Claims Act of 1971.* S. Report 92–405, 21 October 1971.

———. *Alaska Native Settlement Act.* S. Report 92–581 to accompany Conference Report on HR 10367, 92nd Congress, 1st Session, 14 December 1971.

U.S. Commission on Civil Rights. *Staff Memorandum On the Constitutional Status of American Indians.* March 1973. (Mimeographed.)

U.S. Congress. Senate. *Menominee Restoration Act.* S. Report 93–604, 93rd Congress, 1st Session, 6 December 1973.

———. *Health Care Improvement Act.* S. Report 94–133, 94th Congress, 1st Session, 13 May 1975.

———. *The Indian Child Welfare Act of 1977.* S. Report 95–597, 95th Congress, 1st Session, 3 November 1977.

U.S. Department of Commerce, Bureau of the Census. *Advance Reports: 1980 Census of Population and Housing, PHC 80-v–1.* April 1981.

———. President Reagan's Indian Policy Statement. White House Press Release. 14 January 1983. (Mimeographed.)

U.S. Department of Health, Education, and Welfare, Office of Human Development Services. *Indian Child Welfare: A State of the Field Study: Summary of Findings and Discussions of Policy Implications.* n.d.

U.S. Statutes at Large, 1970–1980

Alaska Native Claims Settlement Act (PL 92–203). *Statutes at Large.* 1971.
Menominee Restoration Act (PL 93–197). *Statutes at Large.* 1973.
Indian Health Care Improvement Act (PL 94–437). *Statutes at Large.* 1976.
Indian Child Welfare Act of 1978 (PL 95–608). *Statutes at Large,* 92 (1978).

Index

Abourezk, James, 17, 80–81
Abrogation legislation, 87–88, 91
Advocacy, role in policy making, 36, 40
Agnew, Spiro, 65
Alaska Native Claims Settlement Act (ANCSA), 25–27, 68, 98
Albuquerque Declarations, 65
Alcatraz occupation, 95–96
American Indian Movement (AIM), 57, 96–97
American Indian Policy Review Commission (AIPRC): final report, xx-xxi n.1, 71; views on sovereignty, 40–43, 80–81, 85
Americans for Indian Opportunity (AIO), 98
Appropriations, role in policy development, 85
Area Redevelopment Administration (ARA), 51

Aspinall, Wayne, 79–80, 86
Association of American Indian Affairs (AAIA), 103

Bipartisanship, 72, 86. *See also* Nonpartisanship
Blue Lake, 66–68
Bruce, Louis, 65–66
Bureau of Indian Affairs (BIA): alternatives to dominance by, 49, 53, 56, 109, 112; history of, 100; perceptions of, 56–57, 77, 91 n.1; takeover of, 95–96. *See also* Federal spending

Civil jurisdiction, 44–47
Civil rights, influence in policy development, 19, 93, 97, 108
Cloward, Richard, 57–58
Collective actions, 96. *See also* Indian activism; Social movements

Community action. *See* Community organization

Community organization, role of in policy development, 49, 51, 54–56

Congressional advocacy, 109; limits to, 80–81, 87–91. *See also* Congressional backlash in Indian affairs

Congressional backlash in Indian affairs, 87–91

Congressional committees: role in policy development, 77–81, 89; staff, 86

Congressional delegation, role in policy development, 85

Constitutional mandate, xviii-xix, 47, 111; sovereignty, 34, 40, 45, 47

Contracting, 38

Council of Energy Resources Tribes (CERT), 100–101

Criminal jurisdiction, 44–47

Cunningham, Jack, 81, 87

Dawes Act, 19–20. *See also* Indian lands, allotment of

Deer, Ada, 99

Deloria, Vine, Jr., 6–9, 101

Ducheneaux, Franklin, 79, 86, 89

Eastern land claims, 88. *See also* Land settlements

Economic development, 20, 71–72, 99, 104; jurisdiction over, 100, 104

Electoral system activism, 114–116

Erlichman, John, 66, 68

Federal spending, role in policy development, 56–57, 109, 112

Fenno, Richard, 78–79

"Fish-ins," 96

Friend of the Indian organizations, 102–105. *See also* Paid lobby

Friends Committee on National Legislation, 103

Gaming policies, 46–47, 103

Gerard, Forest, 79, 86

Government-to-government relationship, 71–72

Great Society, 58, 109. *See also* Federal spending; Poverty programs

Harris, LaDonna, 55, 65–66, 69, 98

Hickel, Walter, 63, 65, 68, 79

Indian, definitions of, 10–11

Indian activism, 88, 96, 109

Indian Child Welfare Act, 38, 90, 103

Indian Community Action Programs (ICAPS), 54–56

Indian conventions, role in policy development, 99

Indian country, 5

Indian desks, 49, 53

Indian education, 51–52, 90, 109. *See also* Indian lawyers; Indian leadership

Indian history writing: activist tradition of, 6–9; conventional tradition of, 3–5, 11; minority group tradition of, 9–11

Indian imagery, role in policy development, 83–84, 108

Indian lands, allotment of, 19–20, 102, 106 n.8. *See also* Dawes Act

Indian lawyers, 54–56

Indian leadership, 52, 55–56, 66, 99, 109. *See also* Indian tribes

Indian lobbyists, 84

Indian Mineral Development Act, 90

Indian policy: history of, 111; major legislation and, 12; opposition to, 88–89

Indian policy-making principles, 18–19; legislation over litigation of, 23–26

Indian political goals, 57–58

Indian Reorganization Act, 19–20

Indian Rights Association (IRA), 103

Indian Self-Determination and Educational Assistance Act, 19, 37–38. *See also* Contracting

Indian Tribal Governmental Tax Status Act, 90

Indian tribes, 99. *See also* Indian
    leadership
Interest groups, role in policy devel-
    opment, 72, 90, 105, 110, 112,
    114–115
Intergovernmental relations, 114.
    See also State-tribal relations
Interstate Congress for Equal Rights
    and Responsibilities (ICERR), 89.
    See also Indian policy, opposition
    to

Jackson, Henry, 68, 78–79, 91 n.2
Josephy, Alvin, Jr., 65

Katzenjammer Kids, 66
Kilberg, Bobbie, 66, 69

Land claims, 88, 90, 103
Land Claims Act, 19, 24
Land settlements. *See* Alaska Na-
    tive Claims Settlement Act
    (ANCSA); Maine Land Claims
    Settlement Act
Legal aid programs, 53

MacDonald, Peter, 99, 100
Maine Land Claims Settlement Act,
    25, 27, 82. *See also* Passama-
    quoddy-Penobscot claims
Media, role in Indian activism, 96–
    97
Meeds, Lloyd, 80–81, 87; views on
    sovereignty, 42–43
Menominee, 82, 99; policy toward
    the, 22–23
"Merits of the case" argument, 82
Merriam report, xx-xxi n.1
Montanans Against Discrimination
    (MAD), 89. *See also* Indian policy,
    opposition to
Morton, Roger, 68

Nash, Philleo, 50–51, 63
National Commission on Reserva-
    tion Economies, 64
National Congress of American Indi-
    ans (NCAI), 98

National Council on Indian Oppor-
    tunity (NCIO), 64–65, 67, 69
National Indian Youth Council
    (NIYC), 95
National Tribal Chairmen's Associa-
    tion (NTCA), 66, 98
Native American Legal Defense and
    Education Fund (NALDEF), 98
Native American Political Action
    Coalition (NAPAC), 98
Native American Rights Association
    (NARF), 53
New Frontier, 50. *See also* Federal
    spending; Poverty programs
Newman, Coach Wallace, 70–71
Nixon, Richard, 109; message to the
    Congress, 34–38; personal motiva-
    tion of, 70–71; on termination, 35–
    36
Nonpartisanship, 86. *See also* Bipar-
    tisanship; partisanship

Oliphant v. Suquamish, 45, 89

Paid lobby, 102–105
Pan-Indianism, 57, 59 n.5, 95
Partisanship, 69. *See also* Biparti-
    sanship; Nonpartisanship
Passamaquoddy-Penobscot claims,
    82, 98. *See also* Maine Land
    Claims Settlement Act
Piven, Francis Fox, 57–58
Policy development: access to, 24,
    90; advocacy and, 36, 40; appropri-
    ations and, 85; community organi-
    zation and, 49, 51, 54–56;
    congressional committees and, 77–
    81; congressional delegation and,
    85; federal spending and, 56–57,
    109, 112; guilt and, 77, 84; ideol-
    ogy and, 15–17, 19, 33; Indian
    conventions and, 99; Indian im-
    agery and, 83–84, 108; influence of
    civil rights on, 19, 93, 97, 108; in-
    terest groups and, 72, 90, 105,
    110, 112, 114–115; lobbying and,
    104; presidents and, 61–63; stud-

ies and, 39; White House staff and, 68–69

Policy-making processes, access to, 109

Political savvy, 104–105

Political status, 9, 18, 27, 44, 47, 71–72, 91, 112

Poverty programs, 52–56. *See also* Federal spending; Great Society; New Frontier; War on Poverty

Preferential hiring practices, 64, 66, 86

Presidents, role in policy development, 61–63

Progressivism, 101–102

Prucha, Francis Paul, 3–5

Public policy: models, xviii-xix; process and framework for analysis, xvii; theory, xviii

Reagan, Ronald, policy toward the Indians, 47, 48 n.7, 71–72. *See also* Government-to-government relationship

Recognition legislation, 85, 103

Relocation programs, 22

Restoration legislation, 82, 85, 103

Self-determination, 8, 12, 18–19, 49, 110; definitions of, 31–33; ideology, xix, 64, 71–72, 78, 109; policy-making principle, 18–23. *See also* Economic development; Self-government; Sovereignty; Trust relationship

Self-government, 20, 71

Severalty, 102, 106 n.8. *See also* Dawes Act; Indian lands, allotment of

Social movements, 94–97, 108–109. *See also* Civil Rights

Social welfare policy, 90

Society of American Indians (SAI), 98

Sovereignty, 7–9, 18, 20, 58, 72, 90–91, 110. *See also* Political status; Self-determination; Trust relationship

State and tribal relations, 44–47, 100, 110. *See also* Civil jurisdiction; Criminal jurisdiction

Stevens, John, 99

Studies, role of in policy making, 39

Submarginal Lands Act, 99

Termination policy, 19, 51, 64, 82, 109, 111; effects of, 21–23; public interest in, 27–28

Traditionalism, 101–102, 112–114

Treaty rights, 23–24, 93, 95–96

Trust relationship, 15–18, 29, 35–36, 45, 47, 56, 64, 77, 82, 88, 93, 109–110, 113. *See also* Constitutional mandate; Self-determination; Sovereignty

Urban Indians, 58, 99

War on Poverty, 34–36, 51–52, 55, 109. *See also* Federal spending; Poverty programs

Water rights, 46

Watkins, Arthur, 17, 22, 63, 87

White House staff: Indian access to, 64–66, 69; role in policy development, 68–69

Wounded Knee, 96

About the Author

EMMA R. GROSS is Assistant Professor in the Graduate School of Social Work at the University of Utah. She is a specialist in social welfare policy, women and minority studies, and American policy development.

DATE DUE